FRAC   UERSITY LIBRARY

ARMS TRANSFERS TO THE THIRD WORLD

ARMS TRANSFERS TO THE THIRD WORLD
Probability Models of Superpower Decisionmaking

Gregory S. Sanjian

GSIS Monograph Series
in World Affairs

THE UNIVERSITY OF DENVER

Lynne Rienner Publishers • Boulder & London

Published in the United States of America in 1988 by
Lynne Rienner Publishers, Inc.
948 North Street, Boulder, Colorado 80302

and in the United Kingdom by
Lynne Rienner Publishers, Inc.
3 Henrietta Street, Covent Garden, London WC2E 8LU

Library of Congress Cataloging-in-Publication Data

Sanjian, Gregory S., 1952–
    Arms transfers to the Third World: probability models of
superpower decisionmaking / by Gregory Sanjian.
    p. cm.—(GSIS monograph series in world affairs)
    Bibliography: p.
    Includes index.
    ISBN 1-55587-085-6 (lib. bdg.)
    1. Munitions—Developing countries—Decisionmaking—Mathematical
models. 2. Munitions—United States—Decisionmaking—Mathematical
models. 3. Munitions—Soviet Union—Decisionmaking—Mathematical
models. I. Title. II. Series
UF535.D44S26 1987
382'.456234—dc19   87-15642
                                                                                        CIP

Printed and bound in the United States of America

The paper used in this publication meets the
requirements of the American National Standard
for Permanence of Paper for Printed Library
Materials Z39.48-1984.   ∞

Contents

Tables

Acknowledgments

The author wishes to thank Dina A. Zinnes and Stephen Portnoy of the University of Illinois; Harvey Starr and John Lovell of Indiana University; Karen Feste, the editor of the Monograph Series; and two anonymous referees for their helpful comments. Special thanks are due also to Andrea Stevenson Sanjian of Bucknell University.

Introduction

Conventional arms transfers among nations in the international system have increased dramatically in recent years. Throughout the decade of the 1950s, the average annual export of major weapons (measured in constant 1973 dollars) was approximately $685 million. In the six-year period from 1970 to 1975, however, that total leaped to $3,915 million (Kemp with Miller 1979). Much of this increase is due to the intensified export activities of a handful of nations, yet there are now more nations supplying military hardware than at any time in the past. In the decade from 1973 to 1982, no fewer than fifty-nine countries transferred arms (U.S. Arms Control and Disarmament Agency 1984).

These numbers—the so-called quantitative characteristics of the arms trade phenomenon—reflect only one aspect of the growth in transfers. A second and equally important development—an increase in the qualitative characteristics of exported arms—must also be considered. The practices of the 1950s and early 1960s, whereby supplier states in effect unloaded superannuated World War II materiel, have now given way to the circumstance in which many of the world's most advanced land, sea, and air weapons systems are disseminated with regularity. This tendency raises expectations among recipient states about the quality of the weapons they will be acquiring. It also forces potential donors into supplying ever more advanced hardware whenever the introduction of a weapon threatens regional capability balances. Since each transfer of a highly sophisticated technology reinforces recipient expectations as well as donor obligations, the practice of transmitting qualitatively advanced weapons seems destined to continue.

These figures and trends underlie the need for a thorough understanding of the arms transfer process. Questions that have traditionally been raised—Why do nations export or import arms? What do they expect to gain? What kinds of risks are involved in the policymaking process?—seem now to have even greater significance, which is perhaps why the literature on arms transfers has also grown. This material was reviewed extensively in a paper (Sanjian forthcoming), and produced the striking discovery that much of what must be learned to venture answers to some of the important questions is already known; indeed, theories about arms transfers can even be constructed by piecing together the findings and conclusions of other researchers. This was precisely the approach taken in that essay, and it produced a formal expected-utility model of the arms export process. The model purportedly described the decisionmaking behavior of one country preparing to select an arms export strategy for another.

The purpose of this book is to continue the inquiry into arms export policymaking by testing the expected-utility model. Whereas the aforementioned essay provided an intuitive justification of the model's expected-utility structure and described some of its formal properties, this book undertakes a comprehensive data-based analysis of the model and assesses its real world applicability. What follows, then, is a summary restatement of the model: its assumptions, its mathematical representation, and some of the literature that motivated it. These are the subjects covered in Chapter 1. The remaining two chapters are devoted to the operational and testing procedures attendant to the model, the data analyses themselves, and the substantive implications of the findings.

Because of the particular nature of the model, all of the tests are on the arms export choices of the United States and the Soviet Union. The procedure, very simply, is to derive and operationalize a series of mathematical statements from the model's expected-utility equations and decision rules, and then to use those statements to predict the annual arms trade strategies of both superpowers in regard to selected importers in four Third World regions: the Middle East, the Persian

Gulf, South Asia, and Central America. The tests are performed with data from the period 1951–1976, and decisions regarding the ultimate worth of the model depend upon statistical comparisons of the accuracy of its predictions with the accuracy of the predictions made for three naive models.

ONE

An Expected-Utility Model of Arms Export Policymaking

The purpose of this chapter is to develop an expected-utility model of the arms export policymaking process. The chapter consists of five sections. The first section summarizes those aspects of the arms trade literature that together constitute the stimulus for the arms export model. Only the studies that are most relevant to this research are considered in the review. The next section describes how expected-utility theory can be used to construct the model. Emphasis here is on the advantages of the approach. Both the first and second sections will be kept brief so as to devote more space to the model's structure and applicability. These are the subjects of the final three sections. Sections three and four relay the model's expected-utility components and delineate their inter-relationships, while section five presents some historical examples that highlight the model's real world relevance.

The Arms Trade Literature and the Arms Export Model

Since the mid-1970s, a wealth of books, articles, and papers have appeared on virtually every aspect of the trade in arms. This trend is certainly laudable and perhaps even overdue, but it has not been accompanied by any major reorientation in research method. Historical narratives and single case studies, comprehensive surveys of the impact of particular variables, and lengthy descriptions of the practices of individual countries continue to be the standard analytical devices. There is, of course, nothing intrinsically wrong with any of these approaches; indeed, they are all quite useful insofar as they supply much needed information about the arms transfer subject. What seems to be absent from this literature, however, is any real attempt to combine the information that has already been gained into a coherent theory of arms transfers. This is unfortunate; such an undertaking, especially when practiced on a smaller scale, is entirely possible. In fact, the expected-utility model to be presented below is an attempt to infuse theory into the discussion of arms transfers, and it seeks to do this by relying extensively on the existing literature.

The model profits, for example, from Kaplan's (1975) review of the applicability of three decisionmaking models—*rational strategic, bureaucratic politics,* and *executive capabilities*—to U.S. arms transfers to Brazil and the Dominican Republic. This study is useful because of its explicit consideration of what is normally treated implicitly by most other researchers: namely, the extent to which arms trade policymaking is a rational, goal-oriented process. From the perspective of Kaplan's rational strategic model, rationality is seen, first, as an argument that is warranted, and, second, as something that can be ascribed to the activities of nation-states. The expected-utility model of the arms trade process operates on the same two assumptions, and support for this comes from Kolodziej's (1980) account of arms transfer policymaking at the "national subsystem" level. The actors here are "nation-states and national governmental author- ities," and Kolodziej claims they behave rationally because they choose policies that maximize national interests.

Included among the objectives of Kolodziej's arms trade actors are political influence, strategic security, and economic gain. All arms-exporting countries certainly contemplate these and other such goals as they conduct their arms trade deliberations; however, the investigators of the Stockholm International Peace Research Institute (SIPRI 1971) argue that it is important to separate countries that deliver weapons to satisfy primarily political and strategic objectives from those that export to gain economic profits or a peaceful import environment. SIPRI labels the political and strategic aspirants *hegemonic exporters,* and it is the policymaking processes of those states that are addressed in this project. This injunction has the practical effect of limiting the scope of the model. "Nonhegemonic" incentives for delivering weapons (such as, for example, economic profits) are excluded from consideration not because they are totally irrelevant to hegemonic exporters, but because SIPRI suggests they are less pressing than political and strategic factors. By the same token, the arms trade model is patterned after the activities of the United States and the Soviet Union to comply with SIPRI's view that those two states are the world's most prominent hegemonic exporters. This last point also accounts for the use of data on the superpowers to test the model.

The expected-utility model thus describes the hegemonic export process. It focuses on the United States and the Soviet Union, and it designates political influence and strategic security as key exporter objectives. These initial features immediately lead to the model's next component. Reference to the post–World War II foreign policy records of the superpowers clearly reveals that each nation generally pursues its political and strategic objectives at the other's expense. Of course, not all engagements are zero-sum; mutual interests sometimes encourage cooperative behavior. But even under those circumstances, there often exists some element of competition between the two countries. Arms trade researchers note that this competitive drive also extends to the subject of arms transfers: Mintz (1980) describes a Richardson-type action-reaction process, Schrodt (1982) considers a contagion effect, and Harkavy (1980) talks of geopolitical competition. There is, in sum, ample support for including the concept of competition in the expected-utility model, and this can be accomplished by stipulating that the superpowers will assess the political and strategic implications of their transfer options on each other before finally choosing their strategies.

Competition is incorporated in the model as a constraint: each country's decisionmaking can be constrained by the potential effects of its strategies on the other. Introducing competition in this fashion naturally raises the possibility that the policy options of a hegemonic exporter can likewise be constrained by other aspects of its external environment. The same argument is made by Frank (1969, 225), who maintains that a transfer could be "offset by the negative quality of operational-environmental factors." Frank claims that these negative environmental factors emerge from an exporter's assessment of the total political and strategic implications of a transfer. In some instances, an exporter may improve its position and realize all of its objectives by delivering weapons, but on other occasions the gains an exporter could make by transferring arms may be overridden by the adverse consequences of arms shipments on its environment. Included among the environmental factors that could have a constraining influence on an exporter's choice of policy are (1) the probable behavior of an exporter's competitor once a strategy is selected; (2) the effects of particular arms strategies on regional relations; and (3) the repercussions of a transfer decision on an exporter's relations with the countries of the import region. A rational calculator is expected to take each of these factors into account, which is why they are all included in the arms trade model.

Expected-Utility Theory and the Arms Export Model

The environmental factors are the final components of the hegemonic policy process, so the next task is to translate the above discussion into the language of expected-utility theory. This probability-modeling technique has been used effectively in recent years to investigate various aspects of international politics. Among the more prominent expected-utility studies are Gallhofer and Saris's (1979) account of the deliberations of Dutch decisionmakers immediately preceding World War I, Alpert's (1976) Bayesian model of national capability builders, and Bueno de Mesquita's (1980, 1981) seminal study on war initiators. What makes the expected-utility approach appealing in these and similar inquiries is that it reflects decisionmaking behavior under what Luce and Raiffa (1957) call the condition of "risk." In the context of the arms trade process, decisionmaking under risk presupposes that an exporter can establish its goals (political and strategic gains) and develop policy options (alternative arms trade strategies) to meet those goals. It also assumes that an exporter is aware of the possible outcomes associated with each option, and that it is capable of assigning a value, or utility, to those outcomes. The one thing an exporter cannot do, however, is identify beforehand the exact outcome that will arise from each option. This particular limitation induces risk because it requires an exporter to base its policy decision on the likelihood that certain outcomes will emerge from certain policies.

The hegemonic exporters in this study are assumed to be *risk-acceptant* actors; but, because some decisionmaking settings engender greater risk than others, the arms export model has been developed to fit several levels of risk. What distinguishes one level from another is the characteristics of the import environment. The import environment refers to the prospective importer and all of its neighbors. Two variables that are used to characterize this environment, and that also accommodate the wider concerns of hegemonic exporters, are labeled *regional status* and *regional relations*. Regional status classifies an import region in terms of its salience to both an exporter and its principal political and strategic competitor. When a region is contested by both nations, it is designated as *competitive*, but it is *noncompetitive* when one of the hegemonic powers dominates. Regional relations, on the other hand, pertain to the level of cooperation and conflict among the members of an import region. A region is characterized as *cooperative* when an importer has friendly relations with all of its neighbors, but it is *conflictual* when an importer's relations with any one state are hostile.

Both environmental variables subsume two classifications; therefore, when merged, they produce four possible combinations, or kinds, of regions—*noncompetitive-cooperative, noncompetitive-conflictual, competitive-cooperative,* and *competitive-conflictual*. The level of decisionmaking risk is expected to differ for each of these regions. Regions that are noncompetitive-cooperative, for example, would probably entail a minimum amount of risk. In these instances, an exporter is not likely to be overly concerned about the activities of its competitor, and it can select its arms trade policy with the knowledge that relations are peaceful between the prospective importer and its neighbors. At the other extreme is the competitive-conflictual region. In this, the most hazardous setting, an exporter would probably seek extensive information about the implications of its arms strategies for both regional relations and the relations of its adversary before finally making its choice. The remaining two regions involve moderate levels of risk. An exporter would be especially alert to the effects of its strategies on regional relations when the import environment is noncompetitive-conflictual, but its emphasis would likely shift to the status of its competitor's relations when the region is competitive-cooperative.

The policymaking process for each region involves a particular level of risk, so it stands to reason that there will be some differences between the processes of the four regions. These differences are still captured by the model because arms trade policymaking for each region is represented by a unique configuration of four expected-utility lotteries. The lotteries pertain to an exporter's analysis of relations between various combinations of countries, and they are motivated by the preceding literature review. The first lottery simply requires an exporter to assess its relations with a prospective importer. It is based on the assumption that an exporter will pursue an arms trade arrangement with another country only after first affirming that its relations with that country will be satisfactory. If an exporter is content with the expected course of its bilateral relations, it can proceed to examine the potential effects of its arms trade strategies on (1) its multilateral relations with the importer and every other nation in the import region; (2) the multilateral relations between its principal competitor and every other country in the import region, including the prospective importer; and (3) the multilateral relations between the importer and all of the importer's neighbors. An exporter's assessment of these three multilateral relations is represented by Lotteries 2, 3, and 4, respectively.

The four lotteries are the components of a two-stage policymaking process. The first stage is modeled by Lottery 1 and applies to every kind of import region. There is no conceivable circumstance under which a rational hegemonic exporter would not address something so fundamental as its relations with the importer. The Stage 1 deliberations are also expected to be less exacting for an exporter, requiring only general information about the likely course of its bilateral relations. Stage 2, on the other hand, pertains to Lotteries 2 through 4 and necessitates detailed information about the possible consequences of an exporter's alternative arms transfer strategies. Although both stages are usually instrumental in the process, Stage 1 is critical because it represents a necessary condition for passage to Stage 2. If an exporter is not satisfied with what its relations will be like with the prospective importer, the decisionmaking process ceases, and the Stage 2 lotteries are suspended.

Of the three Stage 2 lotteries, only Lottery 2 is part of the decisionmaking for each region. A rational hegemonic exporter seeking to maintain or improve its political and strategic posture would always examine the implications of its policies for its relations with the countries that may be affected by them. The remaining two lotteries apply only to selected regions. Lottery 3—an exporter's evaluation of its competitor's relations—applies to regions that are competitive, while Lottery 4—an exporter's evaluation of regional relations—is assigned to regions that are conflictual. This division follows from the earlier discussion of the circumstances under which the issues modeled by those lotteries are anticipated as being most important. Of course, all four lotteries undoubtedly have some relevance to the policymaking process associated with each region; but the view is that policymaking for a region can still be approximated by the appointed lotteries. This means, then, that the expected-utility model is actually a collection of four separate submodels. Each submodel describes export decisionmaking for a particular import region, and each consists of a particular set of lotteries. Table 1.1 summarizes this discussion by listing the lotteries and the degree of risk corresponding to each region. The ledger located at the bottom of the table defines the lotteries.

Table 1.1 The Arms Export Submodels

Regional Status	Regional Relations	
	Cooperative	Conflictual
Noncompetitive	Stage 1: Lottery 1 Stage 2: Lottery 2 Risk: minimum	Stage 1: Lottery 1 Stage 2: Lotteries 2 and 4 Risk: moderate
Competitive	Stage 1: Lottery 1 Stage 2: Lotteries 2 and 3 Risk: moderate	Stage 1: Lottery 1 Stage 2: Lotteries 2, 3, and 4 Risk: maximum

Lottery	Description
1	The exporter's relations with the importer
2	The exporter's relations with all of the countries in the import region
3	The competitor's relations with all of the countries in the import region
4	Relations among the countries in the import region

The Expected-Utility Lotteries

The expected-utility model focuses on the policymaking activities of an exporter toward an importer within a particular region. Let A denote the exporter and X identify the region. While there may be N states within the region (denoted $x_1, x_2, \ldots x_n$), country x_i is designated as the importer. At any particular time, t, nation A can select any one of S mutually exclusive and exhaustive strategies (denoted $a_1, a_2, \ldots a_s$) for x_i. Although, in theory, the number of these alternatives could be very large, time constraints, lack of information, and other such inconveniences probably have the practical effect of limiting the range of options A is likely to consider. For these reasons—and also for the sake of simplicity—the common practice of specifying dichotomous choices (Gallhofer and Saris, Alpert, Bueno de Mesquita) is adopted in this study. The expected-utility model is, therefore, an evaluation of two arms trade strategies, with the first (a_1) always more advantageous for an importer than the second (a_2). Strategies a_1 and a_2 are defined alternatively as export/no export, increase/decrease exports, and export high/export low in the empirical analyses.

Any expected-utility estimate must be a function of the probabilities and utilities corresponding to certain outcomes. Throughout the course of this study, the outcomes pertain to political relations between various combinations of countries. Nation A could be concerned about M such political relations outcomes (denoted $r_1, r_2, \ldots r_m$), but these, too, are visualized as a dichotomy; specifically, outcome r_1 describes relations between nations that are cooperative, while r_2 identifies conflictual relations. Since each lottery focuses on a particular aspect of A's decisionmaking involving a particular set of countries, the precise meanings of r_1 and r_2 naturally change from one lottery to the next. Let x_j denote any one of the N countries, including x_i, in X, and let B denote A's political and strategic adversary. On the basis of these definitions and the earlier discussion of the purposes of the four lotteries, the events r_1 and r_2 describe, successively, A's relations with x_i (Lottery 1), A's relations with each x_j (Lottery 2), B's relations with each x_j (Lottery 3), and relations among the x_j states (Lottery 4).

The political relations evaluations in each of the lotteries are always presented from the perspective of nation A. It is, after all, nation A's decisionmaking that is examined in this study. Moreover, the two political relations outcomes in each lottery are assigned the $t+1$ time period. This differs from the time period given to the a_1 and a_2 arms trade strategies (t), but it does emphasize that A's choice of strategy depends upon *prospective* rather than current relations between countries. In Lottery 1, for example, nation A is judging the suitability of delivering weapons to x_i by estimating the probable *course* of its relations with that nation. In a similar fashion, A's purpose in the three Stage 2 lotteries is to calculate the *potential* impact of its two arms trade options on relations between several groups of countries.

One point that bears repeating is the fundamental difference between Lottery 1 and the three Stage 2 lotteries. The first lottery stipulates that nation A will deliver arms to x_i only after establishing that its relations with the importer will be satisfactory once the transfer is made. This is the sole purpose of the lottery. In this first stage of the process, A is *not* comparing a_1 and a_2 to ascertain an optimal strategy; rather, A is simply determining whether one strategy—strategy a_1, which is always defined as *export arms* in Lottery 1—is sensible and worth considering, given the expected path of its relations with x_i. Since this first lottery only concerns the feasibility of one strategy, it is represented in the expected-utility model by a single equation. This differs sharply from the features of the three Stage 2 lotteries. Nation A's intention during those deliberations is to determine its best strategy for x_i. Each Stage 2 lottery, therefore, consists of two equations: the first represents A's expected-utility estimate for strategy a_1, while the second pertains to strategy a_2.

The distinction between Lottery 1 and the other three lotteries is also reflected in the probabilities. These variables record A's estimates of the likelihood of both cooperative and conflictual relations between various combinations of countries at time $t+1$. In the three Stage 2 lotteries (each of which consists of two equations), the probabilities pertaining to the political relations outcomes are always made conditional upon the strategy that is considered in an equation. This construction ensures that any differences between the potential effects of A's two arms strategies are captured by the model. On the other hand, the probabilities in Lottery 1 are not conditional. The first lottery consists of only one equation and focuses exclusively on the a_1 strategy, so there is no need to distinguish between strategies through conditional probabilities. Despite these differences, there is one aspect of the probabilities that remains the same for all four lotteries: the probabilities in each expected-utility equation always add up to 1.

The utilities of the four lotteries connote A's attitudes toward both cooperative and conflictual relations between or among various countries at time $t+1$. Of course, A's utilities for the two political relations outcomes are likely to be very different: A would probably not prefer, for example, both cooperative and conflictual relations between a specific pair of countries at any one time. In a similar fashion, A's attitudes toward r_1 and r_2 may also differ across the four lotteries: A could very well demonstrate a preference for cooperative relations between itself and a particular x_j state in Lottery 2, and conflictual relations between its competitor and the same state in Lottery 3. Inasmuch as many such variations are possible, each utility in the expected-utility model is given a unique interpretation together with upper and lower boundaries that conform to that interpretation. These boundaries may be either positive or negative, depending on the meaning of the utility. A positive upper boundary suggests that A could conceivably favor the political relations outcome covered by the utility, while a negative lower boundary implies that A may oppose that outcome.

Although there are many differences between the utilities, not one of these variables is conditional upon a strategy that is considered in an equation. The practical implication of this proviso is for Lotteries 2, 3, and 4. It means that the utilities for outcomes r_1 and r_2 do not change over the two equations in each of those lotteries. The reasoning here is that nation A's opinions about the suitability of cooperative and conflictual relations between a particular set of states are not likely to be affected by the arms trade policy it is contemplating for x_i. Those opinions are probably motivated by A's own political and strategic relationships with the relevant actors.

Most of the key features of the arms export model have now been introduced. What follows, then, are the seven expected-utility equations that together constitute the model. The equations are presented on a lottery-by-lottery basis, with some discussion of the attendant utilities after each lottery. The reader should note that the subscript outside the rightmost parenthesis of each variable in each equation is a lottery identification number.

Lottery 1: A's relations with x_i.

Equation 1.1 $E[U(a_{1i,t})]_1 = P(r_{1i,t+1})_1 U(r_{1i,t+1})_1$
$$+P(r_{2i,t+1})_1 U(r_{2i,t+1})_1,$$

where

$E[U(a_{1i,t})]_1 =$ A's expected-utility for pursuing strategy a_1 with x_i at t, based on A's estimate of its relations with x_i at $t+1$,

$P(r_{1i,t+1})_1 =$ the probability that relations outcome r_1 occurs between A and x_i at $t+1$,

$U(r_{1i,t+1})_1 =$ the utility that A has for the occurrence of relations outcome r_1 with x_i at $t+1$,

$P(r_{2i,t+1})_1 =$ $1 - P(r_{1i,t+1})_1 =$ the probability that relations outcome r_2 occurs between A and x_i at $t+1$,

$U(r_{2i,t+1})_1 =$ $U(r_{1i,t+1})_1 - 1 =$ the utility that A has for the occurrence of relations outcome r_2 with x_i at $t+1$,

and where

$$0 \le U(r_{1i,t+1})_1 \le 1$$
$$-1 \le U(r_{2i,t+1})_1 \le 0.$$

The utilities in this first lottery have been given boundaries that reflect A's preference for cooperative relations with country x_i at $t+1$ $(0 \le U(r_{1i,t+1})_1 \le 1)$ and opposition to conflictual relations $(-1 \le U(r_{2i,t+1})_1 \le 0)$. The boundaries for the utilities also indicate that Equation 1.1 can be either positive or negative. A positive score favors the importer's chance of eventually receiving arms. It means that A is content with the path of its relations with x_i and is, therefore, willing to continue with its decisionmaking by comparing a_1 and a_2 in the Stage 2 process. A negative score, on the other hand, suggests that A finds its relationship with x_i unsatisfactory, in which case A ceases deliberations and chooses the a_2 default option. These arguments are expressed succinctly by the Lottery 1 decision rule, which specifies the condition under which A would proceed to the appropriate Stage 2 lotteries:

Proceed to Stage 2 and compare a_1 and a_2 whenever $E[U(a_{1i,t})]_1 > 0$; otherwise, select a_2 and suspend all decisionmaking activities.

Nation A's utilities for both cooperative and conflictual relations in Lottery 1 are influenced by the nature of its relationship with x_i during the decisionmaking time period (t). The better that relationship, for example, the nearer the cooperation utility will be to its upper boundary of 1 and, by implication, the greater will be A's incentive to conduct its Stage 2 evaluations. Of course, when A's incentive to proceed to Stage 2 increases, its disincentive—which is represented by the conflict utility—naturally decreases. In other words, as the cooperative utility approaches its upper boundary of 1, the conflict utility should move toward its upper boundary of 0. The relationship specified between the utilities in the lottery—that is, $U(r_{1i,t+1})_1 = U(r_{2it+1})_1 - 1$— ensures that this will happen, and it also permits the impact of the disincentive to increase whenever the incentive to proceed to Stage 2 declines.

Lottery 2: A's relations with each x_j.

Equation 1.2 $E[U(a_{1i,t})]_2 = \sum_{j=1}^{n} P(r_{1j,t+1} \mid a_{1i,t})_2 U(r_{1j,t+1})_2$

$$+ P(r_{2j,t+1} \mid a_{1i,t})_2 U(r_{2j,t+1})_2$$

Equation 1.3 $E[U(a_{2i,t})]_2 = \sum_{j=1}^{n} P(r_{1j,t+1} \mid a_{2i,t})_2 U(r_{1j,t+1})_2$

$$+ P(r_{2j,t+1} \mid a_{2i,t})_2 U(r_{2j,t+1})_2 \, ,$$

where

$E[U(a_{1i,t})]_2$ = A's expected-utility for pursuing strategy a_1 with x_i at t, based on A's estimate of the effect of a_1 on its multilateral relations at $t+1$,

$P(r_{1j,t+1} \mid a_{1i,t})_2$ = the probability that relations outcome r_1 occurs between A and x_j at $t+1$, given that A pursues strategy a_1 with x_i at t,

$U(r_{1j,t+1})_2$ = $(c_{j,t})_2 \cdot w_{j,t}$ = the utility that A has for the occurrence of relations outcome r_1 with x_j at $t+1$,

$(c_{j,t})_2$ = A's relationship with x_j at t,

$w_{j,t}$ = the relative importance of x_j to A at t,

$P(r_{2j,t+1} \mid a_{1i,t})_2 = 1 - P(r_{1j,t+1} \mid a_{1i,t})_2$ = the probability that relations outcome r_2 occurs between A and x_j at $t+1$, given that A pursues strategy a_1 with x_i at t,

$U(r_{2j,t+1})_2 = -(c_{j,t})_2 \cdot w_{j,t} = -U(r_{1j,t+1})_2$ = the utility that A has for the occurrence of relations outcome r_2 with x_j at $t+1$,

$E[U(a_{2i,t})]_2$ = A's expected-utility for pursuing strategy a_2 with x_i at t, based on A's estimate of the effect of a_2 on its multilateral relations at $t+1$,

$P(r_{1j,t+1} \mid a_{2i,t})_2$ = the probability that relations outcome r_1 occurs between A and x_j at $t+1$, given that A pursues strategy a_2 with x_i at t,

$P(r_{2j,t+1} \mid a_{2i,t})_2 = 1 - P(r_{1j,t+1} \mid a_{2i,t})_2$ = the probability that relations outcome r_2 occurs between A and x_j at $t+1$, given that A pursues strategy a_2 with x_i at t,

and where

$0 \le U(r_{1j,t+1})_2 \le 1$

$-1 \le U(r_{2j,t+1})_2 \le 0$

$0 \le (c_{j,t})_2 \le 1$

$0 \le w_{j,t} \le 1$

This second lottery models A's evaluation of the impact of a_1 and a_2 for x_i on its relations with each of the x_j states. Since there are N countries in X, the decisionmaking represented by the probabilities and utilities in the two equations will be conducted N times. Once the individual country estimates for both strategies are obtained, the information is then combined —as depicted by the summation notation—to yield A's overall expected-utilities for the two strategies. Depending on the characteristics of the import region (e.g., noncompetitive-cooperative, noncompetitive-conflictual, etc.), the decision-making process would either progress to one or both of the remaining two Stage 2 lotteries, or come to a close with A's choice of strategy guided by the following decision rule:

Select strategy a_1 whenever $E[U(a_{1i,t})]_2 > E[U(a_{2i,t})]_2$; otherwise, select strategy a_2.

The expected-utility scores generated by Equations 1.2 and 1.3 can also be either positive or negative. Their signs depend upon the boundaries of the cooperation and conflict utilities, and these, in turn, are functions of two additional variables. The first of these variables is $(c_{j,t})_2$, which monitors the level of cooperation between A and each x_j at time t. The variable is comparable to the cooperation utility of the first lottery: it has the same upper and lower boundaries $(0 \leq (c_{j,t})_2 \leq 1)$, and its value will be near the upper boundary when relations between A and x_j are overwhelmingly cooperative.

The second variable of the cooperation and conflict utility functions is $w_{j,t}$, which measures the importance of each x_j state to A. The variable is conceptually different from $(c_{j,t})_2$: it highlights the long-term characteristics of A's association with a particular x_j—such as, for example, the economic relationship between the two countries—rather than the short-term political relations information tapped by $(c_{j,t})_2$. The $w_{j,t}$ variable's mission in the utilities is to act as a modifier, sometimes enhancing and at other times diminishing the impact of $(c_{j,t})_2$ on A's decisionmaking. As will be seen shortly, $w_{j,t}$ is assigned the same task in Lotteries 3 and 4, which is why the variable does not have a lottery identification subscript.

The $w_{j,t}$ variable has the same positive range as $(c_{j,t})_2$. Countries that are minimally important to A register scores close to the variable's lower boundary of 0, while those enjoying maximum importance obtain values of 1. When $w_{j,t}$ and $(c_{j,t})_2$ are combined, they produce a cooperation utility that also has a positive range $(0 \leq U(r_{1j,t+1})_2 \leq 1)$. This range is identical to the one specified for the cooperation utility in Lottery 1, and it is again motivated by the assumption that nation A prefers cooperative relations with every member of X. Of course, the corollary of this assumption leads to the development of the conflict utility. If A seeks cooperative relations with the x_j states, then it would naturally be averse to conflictual relations. What is needed, therefore, is a conflict utility with a negative range, and this is obtained by merging $w_{j,t}$ with the negative of $(c_{j,t})_2$.

This last operation manifests an important distinction between the utilities of the first and second lotteries. Multiplying $w_{j,t}$ by the negative of $(c_{j,t})_2$ means that the relationship between the conflict and cooperation utilities in Lottery 2 is $U(r_{2j,t+1})_2 = -U(r_{1j,t+1})_2$. This varies from the relationship posited between the utilities of Lottery 1 $(U(r_{2i,t+1})_1 = U(r_{1j,t+1})_1 - 1)$, but it accommodates the altogether different purposes of the conflict utilities in each lottery. In the first lottery, the conflict utility was designed to measure A's disincentive to proceed to the Stage 2 process. That disincentive depended on the degree of *conflict* between A and x_i at t. As the level of conflict increased, the disincentive was also expected to increase, so the value of the conflict utility was allowed to move toward its lower boundary of -1. The purpose of the conflict utility in Lottery 2, however, is to record A's concern over jeopardizing its relations with x_j because of its arms strategy for x_i. This concern varies with the degree of *cooperation* between A and x_j at t. The more cooperative the relations between the two countries, the greater will be A's fear of endangering them with its policy for x_i. The conflict utility in Lottery 2 reflects A's anxieties, first, because it attaches a greater cost to the possibility of a conflictual outcome when relations between A and x_j are cooperative (its value moves toward -1 as the level of cooperation increases), and, second, because it restricts A's ability to obtain a positive expected-utility estimate for a strategy for x_i when that strategy is likely to impair A's relations with x_j.

Lottery 3: B's relations with each x_j.

Equation 1.4 $\quad E[U(a_{1i,t})]_3 = \sum_{j=1}^{n} P(r_{1j,t+1} \mid a_{1i,t})_3 U(r_{1j,t+1})_3$

$$+ P(r_{2j,t+1} \mid a_{1i,t})_3 U(r_{2j,t+1})_3$$

Equation 1.5 $\quad E[U(a_{2i,t})]_3 = \sum_{j=1}^{n} P(r_{1j,t+1} \mid a_{2i,t})_3 U(r_{1j,t+1})_3$

$$+ P(r_{2j,t+1} \mid a_{2i,t})_3 U(r_{2j,t+1})_3 \, ,$$

where

$E[U(a_{1i,t})]_3$ = A's expected-utility for pursuing strategy a_1 with x_i at t, based on A's estimate of the effect of a_1 on B's multilateral relations at $t+1$,

$P(r_{1j,t+1} \mid a_{1i,t})_3$ = the probability that relations outcome r_1 occurs between B and x_j at $t+1$, given that A pursues strategy a_1 with x_i at t,

$U(r_{1j,t+1})_3$ = $(c_t)_3 \cdot w_{j,t}$ = the utility that A has for the occurrence of relations outcome r_1 between B and x_j at $t+1$,

$(c_t)_3 =$ A's relationship with B at t,

$w_{j,t} =$ the relative importance of x_j to A at t,

$P(r_{2j,t+1} \mid a_{1i,t})_3 = 1 - P(r_{1j,t+1} \mid a_{1i,t})_3 =$ the probability that relations outcome r_2 occurs between B and x_j at $t+1$, given that A pursues strategy a_1 with x_i at t,

$U(r_{2j,t+1})_3 = -(c_t)_3 \cdot w_{j,t} = -U(r_{1j,t+1})_3 =$ the utility that A has for the occurrence of relations outcome r_2 between B and x_j at $t+1$,

$E[U(a_{2i,t})]_3 = A$'s expected-utility for pursuing strategy a_2 with x_i at t, based on A's estimate of the effect of a_2 on B's multilateral relations at $t+1$,

$P(r_{1j,t+1} \mid a_{2i,t})_3 =$ the probability that relations outcome r_1 occurs between B and x_j at $t+1$, given that A pursues strategy a_2 with x_i at t,

$P(r_{2j,t+1} \mid a_{2i,t})_3 = 1 - P(r_{1j,t+1} \mid a_{2i,t})_3 =$ the probability that relations outcome r_2 occurs between B and x_j at $t+1$, given that A pursues strategy a_2 with x_i at t,

and where

$$-1 \leq U(r_{1j,t+1})_3 \leq 1$$
$$-1 \leq U(r_{2j,t+1})_3 \leq 1$$
$$-1 \leq (c_t)_3 \leq 1$$
$$0 \leq w_{j,t} \leq 1.$$

Nation A's purpose in this third lottery is to evaluate the impact of a_1 and a_2 on B's relations with the x_j states. The lottery operates in much the same fashion as Lottery 2: A will first consider the overall effect of strategy a_1, after which it will conduct a second review for strategy a_2. Owing to the boundaries of the cooperation and conflict utilities [$-1 \leq U(r_{1j,t+1})_3 \leq 1$ and $-1 \leq U(r_{2j,t+1})_3 \leq 1$], A's expected-utility for each strategy can be either positive or negative. Even so, A will still be able to identify an optimal strategy—at least from the perspective of this lottery—by implementing the following decision rule:

Select strategy a_1 whenever $E[U(a_{1i,t})]_3 > E[U(a_{2i,t})]_3$; otherwise, select strategy a_2.

The cooperation and conflict utilities in Lottery 3 are also functions of two variables: $(c_t)_3$, which is a measure of A's cooperative relations with nation B at time t, and $w_{j,t}$, which again weighs each x_j state according to its importance to A. The value for $(c_t)_3$ is obtained once during the decisionmaking time period; it does not change from one x_j state to another. The reasoning here is that if A is to alter its opinion of B, it will do so as a result of a transformation in its relationship with B, and not because of the qualities of a particular x_j state. This means, then, that differences in the values of the utilities across the x_j states depend entirely on $w_{j,t}$.

Variable $(c_t)_3$ ranges from -1 to 1; however, in most instances, its value will be negative, indicating some measure of hostility between A and B. This conforms to the notion that A and B are political and strategic adversaries, and it also suggests that A's utilities for cooperative relations between B and the x_j states will usually be negative. Nation A will simply not want B to develop friendly ties with x_j because of the arms policy A selects for x_i. Of course, when A's utility for cooperative relations between B and x_j is negative, its utility for conflictual relations would probably be positive. After all, A and B are competitors who pursue advantages at each other's expense. If relations between B and x_j become conflictual because of the arms strategy A adopts, then A will have benefited, albeit by precipitating a decline in B's relations. Thus, when the cooperation utility is negative, the conflict utility will be positive, and this is indicated by the relationship $U(r_{2j,t+1})_3 = -U(r_{1j,t+1})_3$.

This explains the negative values for the cooperation utilities and the positive values for the conflict utilities. It probably also describes the typical attitudes of the United States and the Soviet Union. Throughout much of the post–World War II era, relations between the superpowers have been sufficiently antagonistic for each to prefer hostile rather than friendly relations between the other and some third state. There have been occasions, however, when tensions between the two countries eased. Examples include the "Spirit of Geneva" in the 1950s, the Glassboro Summit of the 1960s, and the détente era of the 1970s. Periods such as these certainly do not obligate strategic adversaries to revise their fundamental opinions of one another, but they could induce conciliatory attitudes toward possible cooperative relations between the competitor and other countries. Although the chances of this occurring are remote, the upper boundary of $(c_t)_3$ still takes the possibility into account. Because of that boundary, A's utilities for cooperative relations between B and the x_j states could reach 1, while its corresponding conflict utilities could drop as low as -1. Values for these variables that approach those boundaries suggest that an exporter is willing to accept the occurrence of cooperative relations between its competitor and another country.

Lottery 4: Relations among the x_j states.

Equation 1.6 $E[U(a_{1i,t})]_4 = P(r_{1,t+1} \mid a_{1i,t})_4 U(r_{1,t+1})_4$
$$+P(r_{2,t+1} \mid a_{1i,t})_4 U(r_{2,t+1})_4$$

Equation 1.7 $E[U(a_{2i,t})]_4 = P(r_{1,t+1} \mid a_{2i,t})_4 U(r_{1,t+1})_4$
$$+P(r_{2,t+1} \mid a_{2i,t})_4 U(r_{2,t+1})_4 \; ,$$

where

$E[U(a_{1i,t})]_4$ = A's expected-utility for pursuing strategy a_1 with x_i at t, based on A's estimate of the effect of a_1 on multilateral relations in region X at $t+1$,

$P(r_{1,t+1} \mid a_{1i,t})_4$ = the probability that relations outcome r_1 occurs among the nations in region X at $t+1$, given that A pursues strategy a_1 with x_i at t,

$U(r_{1,t+1})_4 =$ the utility that A has for the occurrence of relations outcome r_1 among the nations in region X at $t+1$,

$P(r_{2,t+1} \mid a_{1i,t})_4 = 1 - P(r_{1,t+1} \mid a_{1i,t})_4$ = the probability that relations outcome r_2 occurs among the nations in region X at $t+1$, given that A pursues strategy a_1 with x_i at t,

$U(r_{2,t+1})_4 =$ the utility that A has for the occurrence of relations outcome r_2 among nations in region X at $t+1$,

$E[U(a_{2i,t})]_4$ = A's expected-utility for pursuing strategy a_2 with x_i at t, based on A's estimate of the effect of a_2 on multilateral relations in region X at $t+1$,

$P(r_{1,t+1} \mid a_{2i,t})_4$ = the probability that relations outcome r_1 occurs among the nations in region X at $t+1$, given that A pursues strategy a_2 with x_i at t,

$P(r_{2,t+1} \mid a_{2i,t})_4 = 1 - P(r_{1,t+1} \mid a_{2i,t})_4$ = the probability that relations outcome r_2 occurs among the nations in region X at $t+1$, given that A pursues strategy a_2 with x_i at t,

and where

$-1 \leq U(r_{1,t+1})_4 \leq 1$

$-1 \leq U(r_{2,t+1})_4 \leq 1.$

Lottery 4 models A's analysis of the impact of its two strategies on regional relations. The important point to grasp about this lottery is that A's decisionmaking centers on the region as a *unit*, and not on the individual x_j states. It is for this reason that the r_1 and r_2 political relations outcomes of both the probabilities and utilities are not subscripted with the letter j. This construction obviously differs from those of the previous two lotteries, but the strategy evaluation process is virtually identical. Nation A first considers the effect of a_1 on regional relations, and then proceeds to an examination of strategy a_2. The condition that must be satisfied in order for A to prefer a_1's effect on regional relations over that of a_2 is represented by the following decision rule:

Select strategy a_1 whenever $E[U(a_{1i,t})]_4 > E[U(a_{2i,t})]_4$; otherwise, select strategy a_2.

The upper and lower boundaries of the utilities in Lottery 4 $[-1 \leq U(r_{1,t+1})_4 \leq 1$ and $-1 \leq U(r_{2,t+1})_4 \leq 1]$ suggest that nation A could conceivably favor or oppose both cooperative and conflictual regional relations. These utilities also lack the kind of complementary relationship that characterized the utilities of the first three lotteries; the sign and value of one utility does not predetermine the sign and value of the other. All of these peculiarities stem from the view that A's attitudes toward both cooperative and conflictual regional relations ultimately depend on how those two outcomes affect A's own relations with the countries of X. If A believes that hostilities in X will be beneficial to its relations, it would probably favor a regional conflict outcome. By the same token, A may wish to impede regional cooperation if that outcome typically frustrates A's relations with the x_j states. Several combinations are possible, including the circumstance that A could gain or lose from the two regional relations outcomes at the same time. The utilities in the lottery are given both positive and negative boundaries, and are allowed to operate independently of one another, to account for all such possibilities.

The utilities are also composites of the effects of cooperative and conflictual regional relations on A's relations with each *individual* x_j state. This conforms to the usual argument that A stresses some states over others during the course of its decisionmaking. And it means that while the utilities pertain to the region as a whole, distinctions are still drawn between the countries of the import region in the utility functions. These utility functions are much more complex than their counterparts in the previous lotteries. They include variables that measure (1) the importance of each x_j to A; (2) A's relations with each x_j; and (3) each x_j's relations with every other x_j.

The Decision Rule Matrix

As discussed earlier, the precise nature of the policymaking process depends upon the characteristics of an import region. Four kinds of import regions have been identified in this analysis, and the policymaking for each is depicted by a particular combination of the expected-utility lotteries. Since the four regions invoke different lotteries, the conditions that must be satisfied for an exporter's choice of strategy also differ across the regions. These conditions are presented in Table 1.2, and are actually composites of the utility-maximizing

Table 1.2 The Decision Rule Matrix

Strategy a_1 is preferred over strategy a_2 whenever:

	Regional Relations	
Regional Status	Cooperative	Conflictual
Noncompetitive	$E[U(a_{1i,t})]_1 > 0$ and $\{E[U(a_{1i,t})]_2 - E[U(a_{2i,t})]_2\} > 0$	$E[U(a_{1i,t})]_1 > 0$ and $\{E[U(a_{1i,t})]_2 - E[U(a_{2i,t})]_2\} + \{E[U(a_{1i,t})]_4 - E[U(a_{2i,t})]_4\} > 0$
Competitive	$E[U(a_{1i,t})]_1 > 0$ and $\{E[U(a_{1i,t})]_2 - E[U(a_{2i,t})]_2\} + \{E[U(a_{1i,t})]_3 - E[U(a_{2i,t})]_3\} > 0$	$E[U(a_{1i,t})]_1 > 0$ and $\{E[U(a_{1i,t})]_2 - E[U(a_{2i,t})]_2\} + \{E[U(a_{1i,t})]_3 - E[U(a_{2i,t})]_3\} + \{E[U(a_{1i,t})]_4 - E[U(a_{2i,t})]_4\} > 0$

decision rules of the lotteries relevant to a region. The first cell of the table, for example, pertains to the noncompetitive-cooperative region. Since, for this region, an exporter's decisionmaking is represented by Lotteries 1 and 2, the decision rules within the cell are the individual rules from those two lotteries. The first rule—that is, $E[U(a_{1i,t})]_1 > 0$—comes from Lottery 1, and describes the Stage 1 condition that a_1 must meet before it can be considered further in Stage 2. This Lottery 1 condition is, of course, required in every arms transfer setting, so it is also included in the other cells of the table. The second rule in the first cell represents the Stage 2 process, and it specifies the condition under which a_1 will be preferred over a_2.

The Stage 2 decision rule for the noncompetitive-cooperative region is relatively uncomplicated because it is only based on an exporter's evaluation of its multilateral relations. In the other regions, however, the Stage 2 rules are summations of the individual rules for two or more lotteries. For example, the Stage 2 rule for the competitive-conflictual region is actually the summation of the rules taken from Lotteries 2, 3, and 4. Of course, the decision to sum the rules is not without risk since it means that an exporter will weigh each of the applicable lotteries equally when deciding its arms trade strategy. Although this is probably not precise, in most circumstances an exporter's consideration of the lotteries relevant to a particular region may still be approximately equal, in which case the specification presented here would be reasonably accurate. This proposition is obviously related to the initial decision to exclude Lotteries 3 and 4 from certain regions.

The Expected-Utility Lotteries and Superpower Decisionmaking

Lotteries 3 and 4 may not apply to every case of arms trade decisionmaking, but there are indications that both the United States and the Soviet Union occasionally make their choices after having undertaken the kinds of deliberations represented by those two lotteries. In fact, the behavior of the superpowers can be used to illustrate the logic of all four lotteries. Consider once more the condition imposed by Lottery 1: an exporter must be convinced that its relations with a prospective importer will be cooperative before it is willing to entertain an arms export strategy for that nation. This requirement is issued as the cornerstone of the policymaking process, even though an exporter's evaluation of its bilateral relations may sometimes be very casual. Relations between the United States and Israel, as well as between the United States and Cuba, are each so sufficiently predictable that U.S. officials need not spend much time pondering the propriety of arms shipments to those countries. Israel virtually always achieves future consideration in the Stage 2 process, while Castro's Cuba does not. Then, too, there are those occasions when the Lottery 1 review will be more thorough. Egypt's 1975 request for U.S. arms must have been gratifying for Washington officials eager to establish friendly ties with that most prestigious Arab state; yet, the lengthy record of hostilities between the two countries undoubtedly evoked a rigorous American assessment of the most likely course of U.S.-Egyptian relations.

The Egyptian example also highlights the multilateral relations approach of Lottery 2. Before choosing its policy for Egypt, the United States surely considered the possible effects of all its arms trade options on its relations with several other Middle Eastern states. Jordan, Lebanon, and Syria undoubtedly figured in the calculations, but the most prominent estimates were probably for Israel. After all, Egypt and Israel were not then friendly neighbors, so a U.S. plan to offer arms to Egypt could have jeopardized the special relationship that existed between the United States and Israel. The United States ultimately decided to supply weapons to Egypt, suggesting that while there may have been political costs involved— most likely in relations with Israel—they were neither sufficiently large nor irreconcilable to offset the political benefits of assisting Egypt. Of course, an arms export solution may not always be feasible, as the United States discovered in its dealings with both India and Pakistan, and Greece and Turkey. In each of these instances, Washington was forced to suspend or postpone overt deliveries to one nation (India, Turkey), partly because of domestic political opposition, but also because of the deleterious effects that the transfers would have had on the United States' relations with the other country (Pakistan, Greece).

The Egyptian case is also germane to Lottery 3. The U.S.

decision to provide military assistance to Egypt was at least partly motivated by the belief that such deliveries would contribute to the decline of Soviet-Egyptian relations and diminish Soviet influence throughout the Middle East. Evidence that the policy was not totally successful emerges from the present tragedy in Lebanon, but here, too, each superpower is operating in a fashion that ensures that its own, and not its opponent's, ambitions are fulfilled. These objectives bear heavily, for example, on the U.S. policy of rearming Israel's occupation force, and the Soviet Union's decision to resupply Syrian troops in Lebanon's Bekaa Valley. Efforts such as these to achieve political and strategic advantages are not at all uncommon among hegemonic exporters. After the United States suspended arms shipments to Pakistan because of that nation's second war with India, the Soviet Union tried energetically, in 1967, to supplant the United States as Pakistan's principal arms supplier. It took several years for the United States to overcome the friendship offensive waged by the Soviet Union and to resume delivering weapons to Pakistan.

One persuasive example of the applicability of Lottery 4 concerns Soviet policymaking in the current Persian Gulf War. Throughout the period of U.S. military support for the shah's Iran, the Soviet Union had been a faithful supplier of various Iraqi regimes. The situation changed, however, once the shah was deposed. The Soviets immediately sought better relations with Iran, even at the expense of their association with Iraq, and they were aided in their quest by the new Khomeini regime's enmity toward the United States. When Iraq decided to invade disputed border provinces, the Soviet Union was given the opportunity of further improving its relations with Iran by assisting that country's war effort. Soviet spare parts were channeled to Iran through both Libya and Syria, and there were also reports (albeit unconfirmed) of Soviet offers to supply Iran directly with vast quantities of arms (Khalilzad 1982, 321–322). The emergence of regional conflict was therefore interpreted by the Soviets as being in their best interests. This is suggestive of positive conflict utilities in the Lottery 4 equations. Since, in this case, regional conflict was more profitable than cooperation, the Soviet Union would be expected to select the arms trade strategy that would perpetuate it. It chose to offer weapons, which in retrospect seems to have been a wise decision.

TWO

Operationalizing the Arms Trade Model

The purpose of this chapter is to prepare the arms trade model for empirical inspection. The chapter consists of several sections, each of which is devoted to a particular aspect of the testing procedure. The first section again pertains to the conditions under which an exporter will select strategy a_1 for a prospective arms importer. The decision rule matrix presented at the close of Chapter 1 reported these conditions for each of the four import environments. The subject of the first section of Chapter 2 is to obtain a series of reduced form expressions of the same conditions. These new expressions become the predicting statements of the model, and the remaining sections of the chapter prepare them for empirical analysis. Section two identifies the actors and cases for which the predictions will be made, while section three summarizes the data that is used to measure the variables of the predicting statements. Alternative methods for specifying strategies, relations, and time periods are discussed next, followed by a description of the indices for the probabilities, the utilities, and the regional status and regional relations variables. The chapter's final section presents a series of naive models that are also used to predict Soviet and U.S. strategies. The statistical tests performed in the next chapter center on the differences between the predictive capabilities of the theoretical model and those of the naive models.

Predicting Arms Export Strategies

The model is tested by using mathematical statements derived from the lotteries and decision rules to predict the annual arms trade strategies of a given exporter for a particular importer. Five such predicting statements have been obtained by substituting the right-hand-side expressions of Equations 1.1 through 1.7 for the expected-utility terms of the decision rules in Table 1.2, by amending the expanded decision rules so that they entertain all complementary relationships between variables, and by replacing the cooperation utilities of Lotteries 2 and 3 with their corresponding c and w variables. The five statements are reported below as Inequalities 2.1 through 2.5. Inequality 2.1 pertains to the Stage 1 process; it emerges from Equation 1.1 of Lottery 1 and the decision rule for that lottery. The other four inequalities are products of the lotteries and decision rules accompanying the four Stage 2 processes. The statements have been presented without the usual time period subscripts as a means of simplifying notation.

Stage 1: All Four Regions

$$P(r_{1i})_1 + U(r_{1i})_1 > 1 \qquad (2.1)$$

Stage 2: Noncompetitive-Cooperative Regions

$$\sum_{j=1}^{n} 2w_j(c_j)_2[P(r_{1j}|a_{1i})_2 - P(r_{1j}|a_{2i})_2] > 0 \qquad (2.2)$$

Stage 2: Noncompetitive-Conflictual Regions

$$\sum_{j=1}^{n} 2w_j\{(c_j)_2[P(r_{1j}|a_{1i})_2 - P(r_{1j}|a_{2i})_2]\}$$
$$+ [P(r_1|a_{1i})_4 - P(r_1|a_{2i})_4] \cdot [U(r_1)_4 - U(r_2)_4] > 0 \qquad (2.3)$$

Stage 2: Competitive-Cooperative Regions

$$\sum_{j=1}^{n} 2w_j\{(c_j)_2[P(r_{1j}|a_{1i})_2 - P(r_{1j}|a_{2i})_2]$$
$$+ (c)_3[P(r_{1j}|a_{1i})_3 - P(r_{1j}|a_{2i})_3]\} > 0 \qquad (2.4)$$

Stage 2: Competitive-Conflictual Regions

$$\sum_{j=1}^{n} 2w_j\{(c_j)_2[P(r_{1j} \mid a_{1i})_2 - P(r_{1j} \mid a_{2i})_2]$$

$$+ (c)_3[P(r_{1j} \mid a_{1i})_3 - P(r_{1j} \mid a_{2i})_3]\}$$

$$+ [P(r_1 \mid a_{1i})_4 - P(r_1 \mid a_{2i})_4] \cdot [U(r_1)_4 - U(r_2)_4] > 0$$

$$(2.5)$$

Statements 2.1 through 2.5 are reduced form expressions of the conditions that must be satisfied before an exporter would choose strategy a_1 for a prospective importer. All that need be done to actually predict strategies with those statements is specify the real world actors (nations A and B, as well as x_i and the other x_j states), determine the characteristics of the import region (to identify the applicable Stage 2 statement), and devise methods for measuring the variables of the statements. Once these steps have been taken, 2.1 and the appropriate Stage 2 statement can then be used to predict whether a given exporter will select strategy a_1 for a given importer. If the requirements of both statements are satisfied, then the model will be predicting that the exporter would choose the a_1 option. On the other hand, the model would be predicting against a_1 and for a_2 whenever the conditions posed by *either* 2.1 or the Stage 2 statement are left unfulfilled. The final step would simply be to check for accuracy by comparing the predicted arms trade strategy with the strategy that was actually chosen by the exporter.

Actors and Cases

The aforementioned procedures will be implemented for the United States and the Soviet Union. Those two countries alternate as Nations A and B in this analysis, and their strategies will be predicted for the years 1951–1976. The arms import partners of the superpowers come from the Middle East, the Persian Gulf, South Asia, and Central America: four regions that reflect considerable diversity on both the regional relations and regional status environmental variables. Indices will be devised that enable the classification of each region on the basis of both variables; but, even without any empirical indicators, it is clear that some sharp differences exist between the regions. The Middle East, for example, would virtually always be characterized as conflictual because of the persistent hostilities between Israel and its Arab neighbors. Central America, on the other hand, would often be designated as cooperative because many of the countries in that region enjoyed friendly relations with one another during the period 1951–1976. The two regions can also be distinguished by the regional status variable. The overwhelming influence of the United States in Central America ensures the noncompetitive label for that region, but the Middle East typically engages the interests of both the Soviet Union and the United States, so that region would ordinarily be classified as competitive. These kinds of differences between the regions are important because they ensure that each of the four Stage 2 decisionmaking processes will be evaluated.

Each region consists of two kinds of nations—*core* and *peripheral*. The core nations are listed in Table 2.1 and are simply the countries for which Soviet and U.S. arms trade strategies will be predicted. In terms of the notation of the model, the core countries alternate as nation x_i for both the United States and the Soviet Union. Peripheral nations, on the other hand, are those countries—excluding the exporter and other core nations—that either share a common land border with the importer or are separated from the importer by no more than 200 miles of open water (Starr and Most 1976). There may or may not be peripheral states associated with a particular importer. Israel, for example, is bordered only by other core nations, while Sudan, Libya, and Saudi Arabia are peripheral to Egypt. The peripheral countries associated with each importer are also listed in Table 2.1, and the significance of these states is that they, along with the importer and the remaining core countries, become the x_j states of a region. The countries that specifically comprise a region, therefore, differ for each importer.

The choice of core and peripheral nations is intended to provide a thorough assessment of the model. The dyads that can be formed, for example, between the exporters and core country importers are indicative of a variety of arms trade relationships. For some pairs of nations (such as the United States and Israel), the preferred strategy should be relatively easy to forecast, but for other combinations (such as the United

Table 2.1 The Arms Trade Actors

Nations A and B: The United States and the Soviet Union, or the Soviet Union and the United States

Regions	Core Countries	Peripheral Countries
Middle East	Egypt	Libya, Saudi Arabia, Sudan
	Israel	none
	Jordan	Iraq, Saudi Arabia
	Lebanon	none
	Syria	Iraq, Turkey
Persian Gulf	Iran	Afghanistan, Pakistan, Turkey
	Iraq	Jordan, Turkey, Syria
	Kuwait	none
	Saudi Arabia	Egypt, Jordan, North Yemen, South Yemen, United Arab Emirates
South Asia	Afghanistan	Iran
	India	Bangladesh (since 1972), Bhutan, Burma, People's Republic of China
	Nepal	People's Republic of China
	Pakistan	Iran
	Sri Lanka	none
Central America	Costa Rica	none
	El Salvador	none
	Guatemala	Belize, Mexico
	Honduras	none
	Nicaragua	none
	Panama	Colombia

States and Jordan), the choice of strategy is considerably less certain. Each kind of dyad is examined in this analysis because a comprehensive test of the model encourages an evaluation of its predictive capabilities for both the obvious and the not so obvious decisionmaking case. The peripheral nations have been defined and included in this study because an exporter is expected to assess the implications of its arms trade strategies for relations pertaining to any country that may be affected by them. It stands to reason that among those countries that may be affected by the exporter's policies are the prospective importer's neighbors.

Data Sets

Three data sets will be used in the empirical analyses. Information pertaining to Soviet and U.S. arms deliveries to the various core countries will be taken from the so-called SIPRI worksheets, an unpublished constant-dollar (1973) valuation of annual arms exports to ninety-seven importers from 1950 through 1976. These worksheets complement the *Arms Trade Registers* (SIPRI 1975), a SIPRI publication that reports deliveries of major weapons systems—ships, tanks, aircraft, and missiles—but which does not attach monetary values to the transfers. The worksheets are preferred over the *Registers* because their dollar value data facilitate measurement of the a_1 and a_2 arms trade strategies when they are defined as increase/decrease exports and export high/export low.

The second data set is the Conflict and Peace Data Bank (COPDAB), an events-interaction survey that is used here to determine the characteristics of the import region and to measure the variables pertaining to the r_1 and r_2 political relations outcomes. The events included in the set are all known acts between 135 countries beginning in 1948, and they have been obtained through a content analysis of over seventy foreign and domestic publications. The COPDAB data have been used extensively in recent years and discussed in great detail elsewhere (Azar 1980, 1982); suffice it to say, then, that the information in the set that is marshaled for this analysis are all scaled and weighted (COPDAB weights) cooperative and conflictual events between the arms trade actors during the period 1950–1976.

The final data set is an Inter-University Consortium for Political and Social Research (ICPSR) subset of the direction of trade data prepared and distributed by the International Monetary Fund (IMF). The data reported by the fund are annual exports and imports between 155 countries (cleansed of arms transfer figures), with the earliest entries beginning in 1948. The information that is contained in the set is directly obtained from the countries that participate in the fund. Each member nation is expected to report its trade with all other countries; however, if need be, the fund extrapolates the figures of a slow-reporting or nonreporting country by using the data provided by its trading partners. All of the information included within the set is expressed in U.S. dollars, with exports valued f.o.b. and imports c.i.f. (IMF 1981). The direction of trade data are used in this study to estimate the w_j component of the utilities, which means that only U.S. and Soviet trade statistics are required.

Strategies, Relations, and Time Periods

The a_1 and a_2 arms trade strategies are defined not only as export/no export in the empirical analyses, but also as increase/decrease exports and export high/export low. One reason for the latter two dichotomies is to provide a more challenging test of the model when a decision to export arms is virtually assured. It is considerably more difficult, for example, to gauge whether U.S. arms shipments to Israel will increase from one year to the next than it is to determine whether the United States will be continuing its deliveries. A second reason is to consider whether the policymaking process varies with the way an arms exporter defines its options. Replacing one set of strategies with another without making any other adjustments in the model obviously assumes that no such variations exist: an exporter would use precisely the same evaluation procedures for all of the strategies that have been proposed. This is an intellectually interesting proposition that deserves the inspection it will get through the specification and testing of multiple dichotomies.

Rules have been devised for all three dichotomies to determine whether nation A has chosen strategy a_1 or a_2. These rules are presented in Table 2.2 and are functions of a new variable, $e_{i,\,t}$, which is simply the dollar value of A's arms exports to x_i during year t. The first rule, for example, pertains to the export/no export dichotomy and specifies a value of 1 for a_1 and 0 for a_2 whenever $e_{i,\,t}$ is greater than zero, but reverses the values of a_1 and a_2 when $e_{i,\,t}$ is equal to zero. Values for the two events can be assigned for every year from 1950 through 1976 when the dichotomy is export/no export, but they cannot be determined for the earliest years of the time frame for the other two dichotomies because both are based on a comparison of exports at t with exports at some previous time. The first year for which a strategy can be identified for the increase/decrease dichotomy is 1951 (or, $t = 2$), and the rules cannot be implemented for the high/low option until 1953 ($t = 4$). The second and third dichotomies also allow for the possibility that export levels from one time period to the next could remain the same. This condition, should it occur, falls under the rubric of strategy a_2 for both dichotomies, presumably because maintaining export levels would not be as beneficial to an importer as increasing them.

Table 2.2 Rules for Strategies a_1 and a_2

Option 1: $a_{1i,t}$ = export; $a_{2i,t}$ = no export.
Rule: if $e_{i,t} > 0$, then $a_{1i,t} = 1$ and $a_{2i,t} = 0$; otherwise, $a_{1i,t} = 0$ and $a_{2i,t} = 1$.

Option 2: $a_{1i,t}$ = increase exports; $a_{2i,t}$ = decrease exports (remain the same).
Rule: if $e_{i,t} - e_{i,t-1} > 0$, then $a_{1i,t} = 1$ and $a_{2i,t} = 0$; otherwise, $a_{1i,t} = 0$ and $a_{2i,t} = 1$.

Option 3: $a_{1i,t}$ = export high; $a_{2i,t}$ = export low (remain the same).
Rule: if $e_{i,t} > \dfrac{1}{3}\sum_{h=1}^{n} e_{i,t-h}$, then $a_{1i,t} = 1$ and $a_{2i,t} = 0$; otherwise, $a_{1i,t} = 0$ and $a_{2i,t} = 1$.

A general rule can also be forwarded for the identification of r_1 and r_2, even though those events describe relations between different groups of countries across the four lotteries. The rule is presented in Table 2.3, and will be implemented for each of 108 three-month quarters that cover the span of the twenty-seven-year time period. Values for the two events are determined for quarters rather than years because of statistical requirements concerning the calculation of the probabilities. These variables will be estimated annually; but, to avoid dependency between the probabilities of one year and those of another, the observations on r_1 and r_2 that are used to make the probability estimates must be taken from a single year. Partitioning a year into quarters ensures that a sufficient number of observations will be available.

Table 2.3 Rule for Relations r_1 and r_2

Definitions: $r_{1,q}$ = cooperative; $r_{2,q}$ = conflictual (neutral).
Rule[a]: if $f_q > h_q$, then $r_{1,q} = 1$ and $r_{2,q} = 0$; otherwise, $r_{1,q} = 0$ and $r_{2,q} = 1$.

[a]This is a general rule that is used to identify r_1 and r_2 for all four lotteries. Of course, the precise notation for r_1 and r_2, as well as for f_q and r_q, differs across the lotteries. In Lottery 1, for example, the notation is $(r_{1i,q})_1$, $(r_{2i,q})_1$, $(f_{i,q})_2$ and $(h_{i,q})_2$.

The rule itself is a function of two new variables—f_q and h_q —which are operationalized by COPDAB cooperation and conflict data. Variable f_q is the sum of the weighted cooperative acts between the members of a dyad in a particular lottery during quarter q. Since the dyad in Lottery 1 is A and x_i, f_q is the sum of the weighted cooperative acts directed from A to x_i and from x_i to A. Variable h_q has a similar interpretation except that it refers to the sum of weighted conflictual acts. Since the rules for r_1 and r_2 are implemented N times in Lotteries 2 and 3 (for each A and x_j dyad, and for each B and x_j dyad), variables f_q and h_q for those lotteries must also be computed N times. The events r_1 and r_2 in Lottery 4, however, refer to relations among all of the countries in region X, so, for that lottery, f_q and h_q are the sums of all weighted cooperative and conflictual acts directed from each x_j to every other x_j, and they are calculated only once during each quarter.

As with the arms trade strategies, the events r_1 and r_2 for both options will be assigned values of 1 when they occur and 0 when they do not occur. The relationship between the relevant actors in the first option, for example, would be cooperative whenever f_q exceeds h_q, so for this case r_1 would be 1 and r_2 would be 0. The values for the two events would be reversed, however, whenever h_q is greater than f_q because this would be indicative of conflictual relations. On those occasions when f_q and h_q are equal, the relationship between the countries could be interpreted as neutral; however, in most instances, there would not even be a relationship because the equivalence of f_q and h_q would be attributable to zero values for the two variables. The event r_2 (which corresponds to the disincentive term of the expected-utility equations) is used to describe this condition because an exporter's arms trade calculations would probably not be positively affected by countries with which it does not have relations.

Observations on both the a_1 and a_2 arms trade strategies and the r_1 and r_2 political relations outcomes will be used to estimate the probabilities of the Stage 2 lotteries. These probabilities reflect A's opinions about the possible effects of choosing a_1 and a_2 for x_i at t on relations involving several sets of countries at $t + 1$. Since nations A's opinions at t would be based upon its past experiences, the observations that are used to estimate the probabilities at t must also come from the past. These observations can nevertheless be taken from several different time periods to allow for various lagged effects on A's decisionmaking. Table 2.4 presents the three options that are considered in this analysis. In the first option, for example, A's choice of strategy at t is based upon the effect that its arms trade strategy at $t-1$ had on relations at t. Option

1, therefore, stipulates that the probabilities are to be estimated with values for a_1 and a_2 from year $t-1$, and values for r_1 and r_2 from the four quarters of year t. The lag for this first option is between the selection of the previous policy and its effect on relations.

Table 2.4 Time Period Options

	Observations on a_1 and a_2 Come from Year	Observations on r_1 and r_2 Come from Year	Probability Estimates Are for Year
Option 1:	strategy $(t-1)$	relations (t)	strategy (t)
Option 2:	strategy $(t-1)$	relations $(t-1)$	strategy (t)
Option 3:	strategy $(t-2)$	relations $(t-1)$	strategy (t)

Indices for the Probabilities

The task of devising indices for the probabilities is simplified by the disappearance of all conflict probabilities from the five predicting statements, and also by the consimilarity of the Stage 2 cooperation probabilities. In fact, only two indices need be discussed: one for the cooperation probability of Lottery 1, and a second representing the various cooperation probabilities of the Stage 2 process. The Lottery 1 probability reflects A's estimate at t of the likelihood that its relations with x_i at $t+1$ will be cooperative. The data needed to measure this variable are the values of r_1 between A and x_i for the four quarters of year t. Observations on a_1 or a_2 are not required because the probability is unconditional, and the time period for the r_1 data is always fixed at t to ensure that the most recent information concerning A's relations with x_i is used for the probability estimate. The index for the probability is

$$P(r_{1i,t+1})_1 = \frac{1}{4} \sum_{q=1}^{4} [r_{1i,q(t)}]_1,$$

where $[r_{1i,q(t)}]_1 = 1$ if event r_1 occurs between A and x_i in quarter q of year t, or 0 if event r_2 occurs. The rule introduced in the previous section would be implemented to determine the values of $[r_{1i,q(t)}]_1$.

This index is relatively easy to interpret: as the number of quarters during year t in which A enjoyed cooperative relations with x_i increases, so too will A's estimate of the likelihood of cooperative relations with x_i during year $t+1$. The index for the cooperation probabilities of the Stage 2 process is only slightly more complicated. Those variables are conditional upon A's past choice of strategy, so data on either a_1 or a_2 must be used in conjunction with the r_1 data for estimating their values. Although the Stage 2 probabilities bear upon relations between different sets of countries (the countries vary across the lotteries), and can be computed for any of the nine possible combinations of arms trade dichotomies and time period options, they are all sufficiently similar that an index for one of them can easily be converted (by revising the subscripts) to any of the others. What follows, then, is the index for the cooperation probability in Equation 1.2, or the probability that relations outcome r_1 occurs between A and x_j at $t+1$, given A's selection of a_1 for x_i at t. The observations on a_1 and r_1 in the index come from the years stipulated in the first time period option. The index is

$$P(r_{1j,t+1} \mid a_{1i,t})_2 = \frac{1 + \displaystyle\sum_{q=1}^{4} [r_{1j,q(t)}]_2 a_{1i,t-1}}{2 + 4a_{1i,t-1}},$$

where
$[r_{1j,q(t)}]_2 = $ 1 if event r_1 occurs between A and x_j in quarter q of year t, or 0 if event r_2 occurs;
$a_{1i,t-1} = $ 1 if A selected strategy a_1 for x_i in year $t-1$, or 0 if A selected strategy a_2.

The index suggests that if nation A had chosen strategy a_1 for x_i at $t-1$, then the effect of that strategy on A's relations with x_j at t would be a satisfactory indicator of what might happen to A's relations with that same x_j state if A were again to choose a_1 for x_i at t. The more cooperative A's relations are with x_j at t, the greater is the likelihood that they would also be cooperative at $t+1$. Notice, however, that the probability estimate would have been 0.5 had A, instead, chosen strategy a_2 at $t-1$. This development also occurs for the other cooperation probabilities of the Stage 2 lotteries. As a general rule, therefore, each probability at t that is conditional upon the strategy chosen by A

at $t-1$ can be estimated by evaluating the effect of that previous strategy on relations at t, but a probability at t that relates to the strategy not selected by A at $t-1$ will always be 0.5. The interpretation in this latter situation is that A would simply not have enough recent information about the political relations implications of the strategy not chosen to make an estimate more confident than 0.5. This means, of course, that the model ultimately becomes an evaluation of the efficacy of A's most recent arms strategy for x_i.

Indices for the Utilities

The utilities of the four lotteries reflect A's preferences at t concerning cooperative and conflictual relations between or among various actors at $t+1$. All of the utilities operate on COPDAB cooperation and conflict data, and those of the three Stage 2 lotteries also rely on IMF trade figures. Use of the COPDAB data underlies an important principle behind every utility—namely, that information on the relationships between countries at t can provide at least some indication of A's preferences regarding cooperative and conflictual relations at $t+1$. This idea is incorporated in the index for the cooperation utility of Lottery 1, which describes A's attitude toward the occurrence of relations outcome r_1 with x_i at $t+1$. The index is

$$U(r_{1i,t+1})_1 = \frac{(F_{i,t})_1}{(F_{i,t})_1 + (H_{i,t})_1},$$

where
$(F_{i,t})_1 =$ the sum of the weighted cooperative acts directed from A to x_i and from x_i to A during year t,
$(H_{i,t})_1 =$ the sum of the weighted conflictual acts directed from A to x_i and from x_i to A during year t.

This first index registers the proportion of weighted cooperative acts directed from A to x_i and from x_i to A during year t. The greater that proportion, the greater will be A's utility for cooperative relations with x_i at $t+1$. The index for the cooperation utility of Lottery 2 operates in much the same fashion. This second utility records A's attitudes toward cooperative relations with the x_j states at $t+1$, and was defined earlier as $U(r_{1j,t+1})_2 = (c_{j,t})_2 \cdot w_{j,t}$. Variable $(c_{j,t})_2$ measures the extent to which A's relations with each x_j are cooperative, while $w_{j,t}$ denotes the importance of each x_j to A. The two variables are themselves functions of other variables as is indicated by the index:

$$U(r_{1j,t+1})_2 = \frac{(F_{j,t})_2}{(F_{j,t})_2 + (H_{j,t})_2} \cdot \frac{T_{j,t}}{\sum_{j=1}^{n} T_{j,t}} ,$$

where

$(F_{j,t})_2 =$ the sum of the weighted cooperative acts directed from A to x_j and from x_j to A during year t,

$(H_{j,t})_2 =$ the sum of the weighted conflictual acts directed from A to x_j and from x_j to A during year t,

$T_{j,t} =$ the dollar value of nation A's trade (exports and imports) with x_j during year t.

Variable $(c_{j,t})_2$ is calculated with COPDAB data and is very much like $U(r_{1i,t+1})_1$. The only difference is that $(c_{j,t})_2$ must be computed N times because $U(r_{1j,t+1})_2$ is estimated individually for each of the x_j states. The same condition applies, of course, to $w_{j,t}$, which is measured with IMF trade data. This variable records each x_j state's proportion of the total trade conducted by nation A with the countries of region X. While $w_{j,t}$ ranges from 0 to 1, nation A must steer most of its trade toward a particular x_j state before the value of $w_{j,t}$ for that country can approach its upper boundary.

The $w_{j,t}$ variable also appears in the cooperation utility of Lottery 3, which describes A's preferences concerning cooperative relations between B and the x_j states at $t+1$. This third utility was defined earlier as $U(r_{1j,t+1})_3 = (c_t)_3 \cdot w_{j,t}$, where $(c_t)_3$ denotes the level of cooperation between A and B during year t. Variable $(c_t)_3$ operates on COPDAB data and is computed only once during each t, meaning that variations in the values of $U(r_{1j,t+1})_3$ over the x_j states depend on differences in the values of $w_{j,t}$. The index for this utility is

$$U(r_{1j,t+1})_3 = \frac{(F_t)_3 - (H_t)_3}{(F_t)_3 + (H_t)_3} \cdot w_{j,t} ,$$

where

$(F_t)_3$ =   the sum of the weighted cooperative acts directed from A to B and from B to A during year t,

$(H_t)_3$ =   the sum of the weighted conflictual acts directed from A to B and from B to A during year t.

Indices have not been developed for the conflict utilities of the first three lotteries because those variables do not appear in the predicting statements; however, indices are needed for both the cooperation and conflict utilities of Lottery 4. These variables describe A's attitudes toward cooperative and conflictual relations among the countries of region X, attitudes that impinge upon the effect that each regional relations outcome has on A's own relations with the x_j states. The indices for the two utilities are functions of three variables: $[c_{j,q(t)}]_4$, which describes A's relations with each x_j; $w_{j,t}$, which again weighs each x_j in terms of its importance to A; and either $[r_{1,q(t)}]_4$ or $[r_{2,q(t)}]_4$ to determine whether regional relations are cooperative or conflictual. Variable $[r_{1,q(t)}]_4$ appears in the index for the cooperation utility, and is replaced by $[r_{2,q(t)}]_4$ in the index for the conflict utility. The index for the cooperation utility is

$$U(r_{1,t+1})_4 = \left\{ 1 / \sum_{q=1}^{4}[r_{1,q(t)}]_4 \right\} \left\{ \left\{ \sum_{q=1}^{4}[r_{1,q(t)}]_4 \right\} \left\{ \sum_{j=1}^{n} w_{j,t} \cdot [c_{j,q(t)}]_4 \right\} \right\},$$

where

$$[c_{j,q(t)}]_4 = \left\{ \frac{[F_{j,q(t)}]_2}{[F_{j,q(t)}]_2 + [H_{j,q(t)}]_2} - \frac{[H_{j,q(t)}]_2}{[F_{j,q(t)}]_2 + [H_{j,q(t)}]_2} \right\}$$

$[r_{1,q(t)}]_4$ = 1 if event r_1 occurs among the countries in region X in quarter q of year t, or 0 if event r_2 occurs,

$[F_{j,q(t)}]_2$ = the sum of the weighted cooperative acts directed from A to x_j and from x_j to A during quarter q of year t,

$[H_{j,q(t)}]_2$ = the sum of the weighted conflictual acts directed from A to x_j and from x_j to A during quarter q of year t.

Variables $w_{j,t}$ and $[c_{j,q(t)}]_4$ measure the importance of each x_j

state to A during the four quarters of year t. When information on both variables has been obtained for all of the x_j states in a quarter, it is summed and multiplied by the value of $[r_{1,q(t)}]_4$. This particular step is an important one because the value of $[r_{1,q(t)}]_4$ indicates whether regional relations during the quarter are cooperative. If they are cooperative, then $[r_{1,q(t)}]_4$ would be 1, and the computations pertaining to A's relations in the quarter would be used in the index. If regional relations are conflictual, however, $[r_{1,q(t)}]_4$ would be 0, and the information about A's relations drops from the index. The same procedures are followed for the other three quarters, after which all of the quarterly calculations are summed to obtain the total effect of cooperative regional relations on A's own relations. That four-quarter total is then divided by the summation of the values of $[r_{1,q(t)}]_4$ to place the utility within its specified range of –1 to 1. Of course, when regional relations for all four quarters are conflictual, the summation of the values of $[r_{1,q(t)}]_4$ would be 0. On these occasions, the index would be undefined; however, $U(r_{1,t+1})_4$ would still be given a value of 0, with the accompanying interpretation that nation A simply does not have enough recent experience with cooperative regional relations to establish either a positive or negative outlook toward that outcome.

Regional Status and Regional Relations

Rules have been devised for characterizing the import region on the basis of both the regional status and regional relations environmental variables. Regional status classifies X as either noncompetitive or competitive, depending upon the participation levels of nations A and B. Let RS represent regional status with dichotomous values 0 for a noncompetitive region and 1 for a competitive region. The value of RS for region X can be determined at any particular time t by simply comparing the total weighted cooperative and conflictual acts between A and all of the x_j states with the corresponding total for nation B. The region is classified as noncompetitive when the total acts for one of the countries exceeds that of the other by a substantial margin, but it becomes competitive when the two totals are reasonably close. Both cooperative and conflictual acts are used in the rule because interest centers on the extent rather than on the nature of A's and B's associations with the x_j states. Weighted COPDAB events are employed because some forms of interstate behavior (e.g., forming alliances) are suggestive of stronger interactions than others (e.g., standard diplomatic communiqués). The rule for RS_t is as follows:

Rule for RS_t: if $C_{A,t} > \frac{1}{3} C_{B,t}$ and if $C_{B,t} > \frac{1}{3} C_{A,t}$, then $RS_t = 1$

(competitive); otherwise $RS_t = 0$ (noncompetitive),

where

$C_{A,t}$ = the total weighted cooperative and conflictual acts directed from A to all of the x_j states and from all of the x_j states to A during year t,

$C_{B,t}$ = the total weighted cooperative and conflictual acts directed from B to all of the x_j states and from all of the x_j states to B during year t.

The regional relations environmental variable classifies the import region as either cooperative or conflictual depending upon the prospective importer's relations with its neighbors. Let RR_i represent regional relations with dichotomous values 0 for cooperative relations and 1 for conflictual relations. The value of RR_i can be determined for any x_i and at any particular time t by comparing the weighted cooperative acts between x_i and each x_j state with the corresponding conflictual acts between the same countries. The region is designated as conflictual if the weighted conflictual acts between x_i and at least one of the other core or peripheral countries is greater then the weighted cooperative acts. Regional relations are determined separately for each importer in X to account for the fact that some countries in a region can maintain cooperative relations with their neighbors even while other countries may be in conflict. The rule for RR_i is this:

Rule for $RR_{i,t}$: if $H_{ij,t} > F_{ij,t}$ for $j = 1, 2,..., n$ $(i \neq j)$, then $RR_{i,t} = 1$

(conflictual); otherwise, $RR_{i,t} = 0$ (cooperative),

where

$H_{ij,t}$ = the weighted conflictual acts directed from x_i to x_j and from x_j to x_i during year t,

$F_{ij,t}$ =   the weighted cooperative acts directed from x_i to x_j and from x_j to x_i during year t.

Naive Models

The material presented in this chapter is all that is needed to predict Soviet and U.S. arms transfer strategies with the expected-utility model. Much of that material can also be used to obtain comparable sets of predictions from three naive models. The purpose of the naive model predictions is to provide benchmarks against which the performance of the original model—hereafter called the theoretical model—can be assessed. The naive models emerge from the theoretical model by introducing a series of simplifying assumptions on the utilities of the Stage 2 lotteries. Naive model 1, for example, simply drops the w_j component from all of the utilities. The model, therefore, proposes that nation A would be disinclined to make any prior judgments concerning the relative importance of the x_j states. The distinctions that A may wish to make between those countries can be captured adequately by the political relations variables—$(c_{j,t})_2$, $(c_t)_3$, and $[c_{j,q(t)}]_4$—of the original utility functions.

The second naive model reinstates w_j and focuses instead on the political relations variables. Values for these variables will be determined empirically in the analysis of the theoretical model; however, in naive model 2, each political relations variable will be assigned a boundary value (either upper or lower) that presumably represents A's actual attitude toward the political relations outcome of the associated utility. In the cooperation utility of Lottery 2, for example, the political relations variable, $(c_{j,t})_2$, pertains to A's relations with the x_j states and ranges from 0 to 1. Since it could be argued that A prefers the best possible relationship with each x_j state, variable $(c_{j,t})_2$ for every x_j will arbitrarily be given the value of its upper boundary. The obverse of this principle governs the selection of the boundary value for $(c_t)_3$. This political relations variable focuses on A's relations with nation B, ostensibly as an indicator of A's preferences regarding cooperative relations between B and the x_j states. One reasonable interpretation in this case is that $(c_t)_3$ should always be given its lower boundary value of -1 in recognition of B's position as

A's principal political and strategic adversary. Finally, variable $[c_{j,q(t)}]_4$ in both the cooperation and conflict utilities of Lottery 4 ranges from -1 to 1; however, under the assumption that nation A always favors cooperative relations and opposes conflictual relations among the x_j states, $[c_{j,q(t)}]_4$ can be assigned the value of its upper boundary in the cooperation utility and the value of its lower boundary in the conflict utility.

Naive models 1 and 2 substantially reduce an exporter's ability to differentiate between countries during the process of its decisionmaking. Dropping w_j suggests that all x_j states are equally important to nation A, whereas specifying boundary values for the political relations variables implies that A's choice of strategy will be unaffected by possible differences in its relations with other countries. Neither of these modifications seems especially reasonable; yet, each is probably more legitimate than the one proposed for naive model 3. This third naive model simply combines the adjustments of the first and second, meaning that *all* differences between countries—as captured by w_j and the political relations variables—are now excluded from the decisionmaking process. Naive model 3, therefore, suggests that an exporter is not just partially inattentive to its foreign policy experiences (denoted by the political relations variables) or to its stakes in the import region (denoted by w_j); rather, the model proposes that an exporter is wholly inattentive. This should have a profound effect on predictive accuracy. Naive model 1 would probably perform better than naive model 2 because deleting w_j is a less extensive revision of the theoretical model than modifying all of the political relations variables, but when the features of both models are joined, as in naive model 3, overall predictive accuracy should decline even further.

Of course, the strength of the naive models rests not in their ability to represent the policymaking process but, rather, in what they reveal about the theoretical model. A comparison of the findings across all four models, for example, should produce plenty of information on both the extent to which an exporter treats the countries of an import region differently, as well as on the factors that are most important to an exporter when making those distinctions. It can also confirm or disconfirm the fundamental premise of the theoretical model—namely, that a hegemonic exporter makes its arms transfer choices almost exclusively on the basis of political and strategic calculations. The theoretical model is constructed entirely of components that reflect such concerns, and it is those components that are in some ways adulterated by the naive models. Then, too, a comparison of the models can also foster more specific judgments about the conceptualization and operationalization of utility in this research: about whether, for example, w_j and the c variables have been brought together and indexed in ways that genuinely capture exporter preferences. These are but a few of the many issues to be discussed during the presentation of the results, which is, of course, the purpose of the next chapter.

THREE

Superpower Transfers to the Third World: Testing the Arms Trade Model

The purpose of this third chapter is to evaluate the expected-utility model by assessing its ability to predict Soviet and U.S. transfer strategies for the importers of the four regions. The chapter begins with the findings on the regional status and regional relations environmental variables. This information identifies the expected-utility submodels that will be used to predict the optimal strategies during the 1951–1976 period. The environmental data are presented separately for each importer in each region, and they are accompanied by some discussion of the relationships between countries in the import regions, as well as between each importer and the two exporters. These brief historical surveys should establish a solid foundation for the second section of the chapter, which is devoted to the forecast accuracy of the theoretical model. Predictions will be made for each of the nine possible combinations of arms dichotomies and time period options described in Chapter 2; the proportion of correct predictions for each exporter to all of the importers in each region will be the first means for reporting the results. Since there are two exporters and nine combinations of arms dichotomies and time periods, some eighteen exporter-to-region proportions will be presented for each of the four regions. These eighteen proportions will then be pared to six by identifying the best time period option for each combination of exporter and arms dichotomy.

After isolating the six best exporter-to-region proportions, the second section of the chapter turns to a review of the

49

exporter-to-importer proportions that correspond to the exporter-to-region results. The aim of this particular inquiry is to uncover any substantial differences in the performance of the model across the various arms trade dyads, and to provide explanations for such differences when they occur. This critique is then followed by an analysis of the four expected-utility submodels. The purpose of this review is essentially the same as that of the exporter-to-importer analyses; namely, to determine whether there are any large differences among the proportions for the submodels, and to account for those differences whenever they exist.

Exporter-to-importer proportions will also be used in the third section of the chapter. The first task here is to report the naive model results for the same arms dichotomy and time period combinations that were found to be the best predictors for the theoretical model. This is then followed by statistical tests on the exporter-to-importer proportions of all four models. The initial test is a three-way analysis of variance, with the proportion of correct predictions as the criterion variable and model, exporter, and arms dichotomy as the three factors. This test, which is administered separately for each region, will determine whether variations in the proportion of correct predictions in a region are attributable to differences among the four models, the two exporters, or the three arms dichotomies. The preliminary expectations accompanying each application of the test are that the differences among the models will contribute significantly to the variation, but that those between the exporters and among the arms dichotomies will not.

The analyses of variance can detect whether forecasting accuracy is significantly affected by the differences among the four models, but they cannot establish whether the differences between particular pairs of models are statistically significant. Such judgments are dependent upon a second test: the Tukey method of multiple comparisons. The Tukey test will be performed on the proportions of all possible pairs of theoretical and naive models for those regions in which the analysis of variance revealed statistically significant differences among the models. The technique is, therefore, used to clarify the findings of the analyses of variance by identifying, for each region, the best model, the worst model, and those in between. After the Tukey results are presented, the chapter will conclude with some comments on the expected-utility model and arms export decisionmaking.

Regional Status and Regional Relations

The first step in evaluating the arms trade model is to describe the four Third World regions in terms of both the regional status and regional relations environmental variables. The findings on these variables indicate whether a region is noncompetitive-cooperative, noncompetitive-conflictual, and so on for each importer in every year of the 1951–1976 time frame. They, therefore, identify the appropriate submodels and predicting statements of the expected-utility model that will be used to forecast Soviet and U.S. transfer strategies for the various importers.   Table 3.1 presents all of the environmental data in summary form.   Located in the far left column of the table (the stub column) are the four possible regional status and regional relations combinations.   Those combinations also happen to be the labels for the four policymaking submodels.   The entries in the body of the table are the number of years for which a particular combination of the environmental variables applied to each importer.   The figures in the column labeled "Egypt" indicate, for example, that Egypt's environment was noncompetitive-conflictual on five occasions and competitive-conflictual on twenty-one. The entries down the columns often differ among the importers of a region because regional relations—i.e., whether a region is cooperative or conflictual—are determined separately for each importer in a region.

The table presents an overall environmental picture that is exceptionally broad, with substantial differences across the four regions and sometimes even among the importers of a particular region. At one extreme is the Middle East, which is consistently conflictual and almost always competitive, and at the other is Central America, which is regularly non-competitive and usually cooperative. Added to these regional variations are some noteworthy differences between the importers of both South Asia and the Persian Gulf. The environments for India and Pakistan, for example, are conflictual on all but one occasion; yet, their South Asian neighbors—notably Nepal and Sri Lanka—usually manage

Table 3.1 The Third World Environment[a]

			Region and Importers						
	Middle East					Persian Gulf			
Environment (Submodel)	Egypt	Israel	Jordan	Lebanon	Syria	Iran	Iraq	Kuwait	Saudi Arabia
Noncompetitive-Cooperative	0	0	0	0	0	1	1	3	4
Noncompetitive-Conflictual	5	5	5	5	5	4	4	2	1
Competitive-Cooperative	0	0	0	0	0	6	9	14	16
Competitive-Conflictual	21	21	21	21	21	15	12	7	5

	South Asia					Central America					
	Afghanistan	India	Nepal	Pakistan	Sri Lanka	Costa Rica	El Salvador	Guatemala	Honduras	Nicaragua	Panama
Noncompetitive-Cooperative	2	2	3	0	3	20	19	21	18	17	24
Noncompetitive-Conflictual	2	4	1	4	1	6	7	5	8	9	2
Competitive-Cooperative	12	1	16	1	16	0	0	0	0	0	0
Competitive-Conflictual	10	21	6	21	6	0	0	0	0	0	0

[a]The entries in the table are the number of years for which the environment of each importer was noncompetitive-cooperative, noncompetitive-conflictual, competitive-cooperative, and competitive-conflictual during the period 1951–1976.

relations that are cooperative. A similar situation surfaces in the Persian Gulf, where the conflictual outcomes registered for Iran and Iraq are counterbalanced by the generally cooperative records of Saudi Arabia and Kuwait. These kinds of variations are not at all surprising; indeed, they were anticipated during the presentation of the actors and cases. Those were chosen with a view toward obtaining large numbers of predictions from each of the four expected-utility submodels, and that expectation seems now to have been satisfied. The data covering all four regions in Table 3.1 reveal that a maximum of 136 predictions can be made for the non-competitive-cooperative submodel, 86 for the noncompetitive-conflictual, 91 for the competitive-cooperative, and 208 for the competitive-conflictual.

The arms trade choices made by the superpowers for the importers of the four regions are intimately related to the environmental outcomes reported in Table 3.1. Those choices are also the dependent variables of the expected-utility models, which means that a discussion of the conditions that led to the environmental outcomes would probably contribute to a better understanding of the expected-utility results. This is the impetus for the remainder of this section. The regional relations and regional status assignments for all four regions will be canvassed in order to place the forthcoming discussion of the expected-utility findings in the clearest possible perspective.

The Middle East

Much of what can be said about the Middle East during the years 1951–1976 is rooted to the Arab-Israeli conflict, an enduring struggle that was responsible for three wars, several superpower confrontations, and a seemingly endless condition of homelessness for thousands of people. In fact, all of the conflictual outcomes reported in Table 3.1 for the five importers of the region can be accounted for by that dispute. A conflictual outcome simply requires a hostile relationship between an importer and one of its neighbors, and that is precisely the nature of the relationship between Israel and each Arab state throughout the 1951–1976 era. Of course, not every instance of conflict in the Middle East involved Israel. Also worth noting were the periodic power struggles between Egypt and Syria, and between each of those states and their peripheral neighbors (Libya and Iraq) for leadership of the Arab world. Those supplementary disputes seemed, at times, to be just as severe as the Arab-Israeli confrontation, emphasizing that the Middle East was a region of multiple conflicts involving a large number of dyads.

Table 3.1 also discloses that the Middle East has been designated as competitive for all but five of twenty-six years, meaning that the regional status indicator has detected a rivalry between the United States and the Soviet Union for influence over the countries of the region for most of this analysis. The only years for which the region is noncompetitive—1951–1954, 1975—reflect lesser levels of involvement on the part of the Soviet Union. That country's direction in the early 1950s seemed to be uncertain. Would it build upon its generally cordial relationship with Israel, even in the face of Western sympathies for the new nation, or would it shift its allegiance to the side of the aggrieved Arab states? Indications are that the Soviets favored the second course, but movement in that direction was stymied by conservative Arab monarchies worried about the implications of Soviet political and material assistance. This situation continued until 1955, whereupon Egypt's new revolutionary regime purchased arms from Czechoslovakia. This was one of the first Soviet-sponsored arms agreements with the Third World, and it precipitated a series of events—U.S. cancellation of the Aswan Dam project, the Suez Canal crisis—that paved the way for twenty years of uninterrupted Soviet activity in Middle East affairs.

The change in the region's status in 1975 happened that time to be at the expense of the Soviet Union. Soon after the October 1973 War, Egypt decided that the United States was the only country capable of extracting territorial concessions from Israel. The Egyptians, therefore, chose to expel virtually all Soviet advisors, presumably as an expression of their faith in the United States' good offices. Even the Syrians—longtime coadjutors of the Soviets—flirted with the Egyptian precedent by substantially reducing the number of Soviet personnel in their country, and by beginning the process of normalizing relations with the United States. The deteriorating Soviet position, coupled with increased U.S. influence in both Egypt and Syria, explains the shift in the region's status from competitive to noncompetitive in 1975. That the region reverted to competitive in 1976 demonstrates that relations between the United States and Syria never really came to fruition. The Soviet Union was able to revitalize its friendship with the Syrian government (Ambrose 1985; Campbell 1972; Lenczowski 1981; Sella 1981).

The Persian Gulf

The Persian Gulf has always been plagued by the kinds of problems that torment most Third World regions: intermittent conflicts between region members over borders and access routes; fractious internal disputes that often lead to coups; and superpower stratagems for influence and control. These are typically the characteristics of an unstable region, and they account for many of the environmental outcomes reported in Table 3.1. The data in that table reveal that the gulf was competitive far more often than it was noncompetitive, but they also disclose that many of the gulf states experienced cooperative relations with their neighbors. In fact, amid all of the instability that is normally associated with Persian Gulf politics is the intriguing finding that cooperative regional relations occurred more regularly during the 1951–1976 period than conflictual. This unexpected discovery means that a large portion of the predictions for the gulf will be made via the two cooperative submodels (especially the competitive-cooperative), and those are the submodels that are not considered in the Middle East.

One factor that contributed to the conflicts in the region was the characteristic differences between the regimes. The conservative Islamic monarchies in Saudi Arabia and Kuwait contrasted sharply with the flamboyant secular one of the shah's Iran, and an even more dramatic distinction existed between the governments of those three states and the various revolutionary regimes of Iraq. These surface differences generated palpably diverse foreign policy concerns and ambitions. Saudi Arabia's objectives were to foster Arab solidarity against "Zionist intrusion," and to sustain economic growth according to the principles of a Western model but without its socially contaminating influences. The Saudis were also vehemently anticommunist

—a response to the atheism of Marxism-Leninism—and that drew them closer to the United States. As the Saudis discovered, however, their partnership with the United States was anything but agreeable to Egypt and Iraq, adjacent states that were closely aligned with the Soviet Union. Most of Saudi Arabia's conflicts were with those two countries; although the disputes never became physical, they were occasionally very heated (Anthony 1981; Haass 1981).

Kuwait's concerns were similar to those of Saudi Arabia, although the country was not nearly as anticommunist. Its principal objectives were to deflect Iraq's territorial claims and to maintain the monarchy in the face of revolutionary Arab movements. Kuwait's troubles with Iraq began in 1961 when Britain granted the former full independence. The Iraqis had long argued that Kuwait was actually their southernmost province. They thus threatened to annex the country, but their designs were immediately thwarted by the appearance of British and Saudi Arabian troops. Iraq had little recourse but to finally acknowledge Kuwait's independence in 1963; however, in recognition of Iraq's continuing menace—both directly and through its support of Kuwaiti revolutionaries—Saudi forces remained in Kuwait until 1972 (Anthony).

Kuwait's conflicts were usually with Iraq, but most of Iraq's problems were with Syria and Iran. Its troubles with Syria were manifestations of the competition between those two states, as well as with Egypt, for supremacy in the Arab world. They were political contests that never resulted in armed conflict. Iraq's quarrels with Iran were both political and territorial, with the severity of the political differences contributing to the ardency of the territorial claims. The dispute festered throughout the 1950s and 1960s, during which time a series of coups and counter coups in both countries produced governments that only rarely had compatible political orientations. Two additional factors that exacerbated tensions in the 1970s were Iraq's claim of sovereignty over the entire Shatt al-Arab estuary and Iran's assistance of Kurdish rebels in Iraq. It was not until 1975 that a detente was arranged between the two states. In return for an end of Iran's support of the Kurdish rebellion, Iraq accepted Iran's position that the boundary between them was the deep-water line in the Shatt al-Arab (Ramazani 1975; Agwani 1978).

Despite the intermittent upheavals in Persian Gulf politics, both the United States and the Soviet Union exercised some influence over the countries of the region for most of the 1951–1976 period. The only years for which the region was noncompetitive were the early 1950s (1951–1952, 1954) and the middle 1970s (1973–1974), periods in which U.S. policy was more assertive and Soviet policy was more reactive. In the early 1950s, the Soviet Union had not yet established a client relationship with any of the gulf states, as it would later do with Iraq. The United States, on the other hand, was lobbying for an anti-Soviet military alliance, was intimately involved in the turmoil that returned the shah to Iran, and had begun to strengthen its economic and political ties with Saudi Arabia. These were the precedents for the more than two and one-half decades of widespread U.S. participation in regional affairs, an involvement so extensive that the United States delivered weapons at one time or another to each of the four gulf importers (Chubin 1982).

Most of the Soviet Union's arms transfers were to Iraq. The relationship between the two countries was generally very good after Iraq's Hashemite dynasty was overthrown in 1958; however, in the middle 1970s, Iraq abruptly reduced its ties with the Soviet Union and gradually increased its trade and political contracts with the United States. Iraq's disaffection toward the Soviet Union grew out of its perception that Moscow had abetted attempts by Communists in Iraq to infiltrate the armed forces. The strain created in the relationship by this event was not then severe enough to affect Iraq's arms dependence on the Soviet Union, but it is reflected in this study by the noncompetitive designations for 1973 and 1974. The region became competitive again in 1975, partly because the Soviet Union managed to resolve its tiff with Iraq, but also because it found another arms client in Kuwait. The Kuwaitis were so concerned about the activities of antigovernment rebels in their country that they themselves acquired arms from the Soviet Union—the principal manufacturer of the rebels' arms (Chubin 1982; McLaurin 1977).

South Asia

Table 3.1 also presents the regional status and regional relations findings for the five South Asian importers. The information in the table reveals that South Asia was very much like the Persian Gulf. The region was competitive more often than it was noncompetitive, and there were also a number of occasions during the twenty-six-year period when some of the importers enjoyed cooperative relations with their neighbors. Then, too, there were India and Pakistan. These countries almost always experienced conflictual relations; and, more often than not, their troubles were with each other. In its ethnic and religious aspects, the Indo-Pakistani conflict predated the 1947 division of British India into Muslim Pakistan and Hindu India. But the enmity between the two peoples intensified after independence, with successive wars in 1948 and 1965 over the disputed Indian province of Kashmir, and with the 1971 war that led to the birth of Bangladesh out of what was formerly East Pakistan.

The machinations of the superpowers, as well as India's border clashes with the People's Republic of China, also contributed to the conflict between India and Pakistan. The South Asian environment has been designated noncompetitive in the early 1950s (1951–1952, 1954), a period in which the United States managed to outmaneuver the Soviet Union on most of the region's political fronts. It was during these years, for example, that the United States was able to recruit both India and Pakistan in the East-West struggle, initially by providing military assistance to India, and then by obtaining Pakistan's membership in the 1955 Baghdad Pact. Of course, that defensive alliance was also the undoing of U.S. South Asian policy. India was so outraged by Pakistan's receipt of U.S. arms under terms of the pact that it immediately asked the Soviet Union to supplement the military equipment it had received from the United States. This marks the beginning of a lengthy period in which the South Asian environment is classified as competitive. It was an era in which both superpowers delivered weapons to India—ostensibly because of that nation's border skirmishes with the People's Republic of China—and one in which the United States continued to supply arms to Pakistan (Barnds 1972; Choudhury 1968).

The next change in the region's status occurred in 1967. In that year, the United States suspended arms shipments to Pakistan, something it had promised to do two years before when it ceased deliveries to India as a result of the second Kashmir war. India's response to the embargo had been to rely exclusively on the Soviet Union for its weapons needs and, to the dismay of the United States, Pakistan followed suit. These events represented the low point in U.S. relations with both countries, and they account for the noncompetitive label that emerged for the region in 1967. The region once again became competitive after that year, but it was not until 1971 and the Bangladesh war that Pakistan finally backed away from its uncertain friendship with the Soviet Union and returned to the United States for its military supplies (Burke 1973; Chawla 1976).

Afghanistan was the only other South Asian importer that experienced serious conflicts during the 1951–1976 period, and its troubles happened also to be with Pakistan. The dispute between the two countries centered on the status of several of Pakistan's northern states: Afghanistan insisted that those territories should either be independent or, better still, incorporated into Afghanistan. Pakistan consistently rejected those demands, and the hostilities that surfaced were ordinarily the result of Afghan, Indian, and occasional Soviet efforts to incite rebellion among the northern state inhabitants. India's support for Afghanistan on this issue was predicated on its own struggle with Pakistan. The Soviet Union sided with Afghanistan, partly because of the special relationship that existed between the two countries, and also because it was partial to India's preferences. In one sense, then, Afghanistan was the beneficiary of the Soviet Union's regional policies and ambitions, and it worked that condition to its advantage throughout the twenty-six-year period as it received much of its economic and military aid from Moscow (Burke; Chawla; Choudhury).

The conflictual relations of India, Pakistan, and Afghanistan stand in marked contrast to the substantially more cooperative records established by Sri Lanka and Nepal. Sri Lanka's only difficulty was with India, and it revolved around the status of about one million ethnic Indian Laborers who had been in Sri Lanka for several decades. Neither country seemed willing to grant those individuals citizenship, so they remained legally stateless until agreements were reached in 1964 and 1974 that fixed definite quotas of Sri Lankan citizenship and Indian repatriation. Nepal's troubles, on the other hand, stemmed largely from its position as a buffer state between India and China. The country tried scrupulously to orchestrate friendly relations with the two South Asian giants, but it could not always avoid becoming embroiled in their dispute. Nepal did join Sri Lanka, however, in fashioning profitable relationships with the United States and the Soviet Union. The two South Asian states received economic assistance from both superpowers, and Sri Lanka even managed to acquire Soviet and U.S. arms in the 1970s to suppress internal uprisings (Burke; Chawla).

Central America

The activity levels of the United States and the Soviet Union in the first three regions were approximately equal. The same cannot be said, however, for Central America. Table 3.1 reveals that the regional status indicator for this fourth region is consistently noncompetitive, a development that is perfectly understandable, given U.S. domination of the Central American political scene in the 1951–1976 era. This finding means that only the noncompetitive-cooperative and noncompetitive-conflictual submodels of the expected-utility model will be analyzed with the Central American cases. Although this might seem to be an unfortunate limitation, it is actually very desirable. Those two submodels are the ones that would be implemented least often in the first three regions, so their extensive use for Central America means that they, too, can be fully evaluated.

Cooperation was more common than conflict among the Central American republics, but the six importers still had their share of territorial and philosophical disputes. One especially notorious incident that fits into the second category was the participation of the right-wing governments of Honduras and Nicaragua in the CIA operation that removed Jacobo Arbenz's leftist regime from Guatemala. That event occurred in 1953 and probably ranks (at least over the years covered in this study) as the harshest example of U.S. determination to fashion Central American governments to its liking. For the most part, those governments only had to demonstrate their anticommunist credentials to receive support from the United States, and weapons transfers—designed to prevent indigenous revolutionary movements from toppling the pro-U.S. regimes—were the key features of that support. The only Central American state that did not receive arms from the United States during the 1951–1976 period was Costa Rica, and that country did not even have a military (LaFeber 1984; Hayes 1982).

Two U.S. favorites in the region were Nicaragua and Honduras, and they also happened to be the chief protagonists in many of the region's conflicts. Sometimes the disputes were between them: Nicaragua's claim to Honduran-held territory led to a series of border clashes in the late 1950s and early 1960s. At other times, however, one or the other of the two states would find itself in trouble with some third state. The infamous "Soccer War" between Honduras and El Salvador in 1969 (which was actually over the status of several hundred thousand Salvadoran farmworkers in Honduras) left more than 4,000 soldiers and civilians dead in the initial five days of fighting. A number of confrontations also occurred between Costa Rica and the various Somoza regimes of Nicaragua. Costa Rica accused Nicaragua in 1955 of training Costa Rican rebels for an invasion of its country, and the long-standing feud between the two nations led to border skirmishes in both the 1950s and 1960s. All of this may be instructive as to the instigators of Central American's conflicts; but, once those conflicts began, even neutral states would eventually be dragged in as supplementary disputants. Costa Rica, Guatemala, and Panama often found themselves in that position (Ameringer 1982; Kramer 1982; Woodward 1976).

The Theoretical Model

This section is devoted entirely to the forecast accuracy of the theoretical model. The first task is to predict the arms trade strategies of the United States and the Soviet Union on the basis of all nine probability options, and then to identify the best time period option for each combination of exporter and arms dichotomy. Table 3.2 reports the results of this analysis for each of the four Third World regions. The figures presented in the table are exporter-to-region proportions, or the proportion of times that the theoretical model predicted the correct strategy of each exporter to all of the importers within each region. The N for any particular cell of the table refers to the number of strategies that were predicted for the exporter and probability

Table 3.2 Proportion of Correct Predictions for Theoretical Model (Exporter-to-Region)

Arms Trade Strategies	Time Period Options	Region and Exporter							
		Middle East				Persian Gulf			
		USA	N	USSR	N	USA	N	USSR	N
Export/No Export	t1	.862*	130	.892*	130	.827*	104	.875	104
	t2	.823	130	.892*	130	.808	104	.894*	104
	t3	.792	125	.880	125	.740	100	.880	100
Increase/Decrease	t1	.696	125	.760	125	.750*	100	.820	100
	t2	.712*	125	.768*	125	.700	100	.820	100
	t3	.708	120	.700	120	.740	96	.833*	96
High/Low	t1	.750	120	.767	120	.802*	96	.833*	96
	t2	.758*	120	.775*	120	.802*	96	.833*	96
	t3	.661	115	.739	115	.717	92	.826	92

Arms Trade Strategies	Time Period Options	Region and Exporter							
		South Asia				Central America			
		USA	N	USSR	N	USA	N	USSR	N
Export/No Export	t1	.854*	130	.808	130	.532	156	.968*	156
	t2	.800	130	.831*	130	.474	156	.968*	156
	t3	.784	125	.800	125	.533*	150	.967	150
Increase/Decrease	t1	.760	125	.680	125	.540	150	.967*	150
	t2	.776*	125	.712	125	.480	150	.967*	150
	t3	.767	120	.725*	120	.542*	144	.965	144
High/Low	t1	.775	120	.750	120	.618*	144	.965*	144
	t2	.783*	120	.783*	120	.528	144	.965*	144
	t3	.713	115	.750	115	.551	138	.964	138

*Largest proportion for the three time-period options.

option that coincide with the cell. The Ns are also exporter-to-region aggregates. They vary across the cells of the table because each combination of arms dichotomy and time period option necessitates a definite and sometimes different beginning date for the first prediction.

The probability options refer to the nine possible combinations of arms trade dichotomies and time period options for which the probabilities have been estimated. The arms dichotomies define the a_1 and a_2 transfer strategies, while the time period options specify the years from which data on a_1, a_2, r_1, and r_2 are taken for the computation of the probabilities. In the first cell, for example, strategies a_1 and a_2 are defined as export and no export, and the data for the probability estimates are obtained according to time period option 1 ($t1$). Since that option specifies that nation A's choice of strategy at t depends upon the effect that its strategy at $t-1$ had on relations at t, the probabilities are computed with the values of a_1 and a_2 at $t-1$ and the values of r_1 and r_2 at t. The theoretical model is, therefore, being used in that cell to predict whether the United States will export or not export to each Middle Eastern country at time t, and the probabilities for that prediction will be based upon whether either of those two strategies at time $t-1$ produced cooperative or conflictual relations between certain sets of countries (depending upon the lottery) at time t.

The starred proportions that are scattered throughout the table are simply the largest from among those computed for the three time period options corresponding to a particular combination of region, exporter, and arms dichotomy. These proportions are, therefore, indicative of the most effective time period options for calculating the probabilities. Of course, for a few region, exporter, and arms dichotomy combinations, the largest proportions are obtained for both time period options 1 and 2. Stars are assigned to each proportion when such ties occur.

Even the most cursory examination of Table 3.2 reveals that there is both consistency and inconsistency across the results. The clearest pattern of consistency is exhibited over the findings for the Middle East, the Persian Gulf, and South Asia. The proportions obtained for each of these regions are usually larger than .700 and often above .800, so they certainly suggest that the theoretical model is functioning very well.

Then there are the results for Central America. The proportions for the United States and the six Central American importers are barely above .500 and sometimes even below it. In short, they are not the kinds of figures that inspire much confidence in the theoretical model, nor are they tempered by the findings for the Soviet Union. The proportions for that country are much larger, but they are also much less meaningful because the Soviet Union never delivered weapons to any of the Central American states. In fact, there are just two very narrow reasons for conducting the Soviet-Central American analyses: (1) to determine whether the theoretical model can predict correctly even when the strategic choice may be obvious; and (2) to ensure that comparable sets of analyses are performed for all four regions. Since never more than five predictions are incorrect in any of the Soviet-Central America cells, it seems as though the theoretical model can predict obvious arms transfer strategies (at least under some circumstances). But even this relatively happy outcome cannot disguise the dismal findings for the United States. Given the significance of that exporter to the region's trade in arms, the results for Central America must be termed a disappointment, worthy of special treatment in the remainder of this chapter.

The Middle East, the Persian Gulf, and South Asia

Among the many similarities in the findings for the first three regions are the performances for the three time period options. Option 2 usually generates the best results (see the starred proportions in Table 3.2), followed, in order, by options 1 and 3. At first glance, this finding would appear to be genuinely useful; it is, after all, suggestive of the periods to which an exporter is likely to turn in order to acquire the information it needs (on the effects of its past strategies) to make its arms trade decisions. Upon closer examination, however, it becomes clear that the above pecking order should not be overstated. The difficulty, very simply, is that for each combination of exporter and arms dichotomy, the differences among the proportions for the three time period options are not especially large. In fact, a survey of the figures in Table 3.2 for all three regions reveals that the largest discrepancy is between the .758 obtained for option 2 and the high/low dichotomy of the United States and the Middle East, and the corresponding .661 garnered for option 3.

The absence of any substantial differences among the proportions for the three time period options is both an interesting and unexpected finding. It is interesting because it indicates that the values of the a_1 and a_2 arms trade options and the r_1 and r_2 political relations outcomes remain steady over a one- or two-year period. If this were not the case, then the probability estimates obtained on the basis of one time period option would be considerably different from the estimates drawn from another, and those distinctions would produce substantially greater variations in the predicted strategies. None of this seems to have happened, at least not on a large scale; quite frankly, the correspondence among the proportions for the three time period options is not especially astonishing insofar as it is attributable to the exporters choosing the same strategies year after year. The typical practice of both the United States and the Soviet Union over the course of the twenty-six-year period was to establish client states in each region and then nurture political relationships with those countries by delivering weapons to them on a fairly regular basis. This accounts for the continuity of the arms trade choices. But, the similarities among the proportions for the three time period options must also be due to constancy in the political relations outcomes. In other words, the relationships between states at time t were very often the same as they were at time $t - 1$. When interest centers on something like the Indo-Pakistani conflict or the long-term friendship between the United States and Israel, the notion of enduring political relations outcomes seems perfectly reasonable. However, for each example of a relatively durable relationship, there were many other instances of fluctuating relations and shifting alignments not only among region members, but also between those states and the superpowers: the periodic scraps between Saudi Arabia and Iraq over the status of Kuwait; the intermittent squabbles between Egypt and Syria for leadership of the Arab world; the uncertain friendship between both the United States and India and the Soviet Union and Pakistan. These are just a few of the many inconsistent relationships between states that ought to have engendered greater fluidity in the political relations outcomes; but they did not, at least not on the scale expected, which means that the occasional perturbations in the relationships between states were effectively overwhelmed by the fundamental qualities (i.e., basically friendly or hostile) of those relationships. Inasmuch as those qualities help generate predictions that are largely correct, the superpowers themselves must have ignored the political relations perturbations as they chose their arms transfer strategies. This finding is entirely consistent with the behavior patterns expected of hegemonic exporters, even though the steadiness of the r_1 and r_2 political relations outcomes is still somewhat of a surprise.

Although it is impossible to state with conviction that one time period option functions better than the others, it nevertheless remains interesting that the smallest proportions are often associated with option 3. What sets this third option apart from the other two is the time period for the exporter's past strategies. Option 3 proposes that information on a_1 and a_2 should be taken from $t - 2$, while the first and second options measure those events at $t - 1$. Since the proportions obtained for option 3 are generally the smallest, a two-year lag between the decision time and the exporter's past strategies is probably too extensive. This conforms to the venerable theoretical argument that decisionmaking information will either be lost or replaced as time passes. It also tempers the above finding of fairly rigid superpower export patterns. The United States and the Soviet Union may be inattentive to political disruptions within a one-year period (from $t - 1$ to t), but their interest begins to surface as the lag time extends to two years. Thus, in arms trade decisionmaking, as in other areas of international politics, an actor's most recent experiences appear to have the greatest impact on its policy choices.

Another point of consistency in Table 3.2 is the considerable correspondence between the results for the United States and the Soviet Union. The greatest discrepancy among the starred proportions is between the .833 obtained for the increase/decrease dichotomy of the Soviet Union and the Persian Gulf, and the corresponding .750 registered for the United States. This difference is not especially large, and since all of the other comparisons between the exporters yield even smaller differences, it appears that the theoretical model performs just as well for one exporter as it does for the other. In fact, the differences that are detectable are probably less a function of the applicability of the model to each exporter as they are a reflection of the cases selected for analysis. These have been chosen to ensure that the theoretical model would be treated with a wide variety of exporter-to-importer arms trade relationships. Some of these relationships are relatively obvious: the United States delivered weapons to Israel in all but two of the twenty-six years; the Soviet Union never exported to Israel, but it did transfer arms to Egypt in twenty-one of the twenty-six years. The complete record covering all three regions is presented in Table 3.3, which reports the number of years that both the United States and the Soviet Union chose the *export, increase exports,* and *export high* strategies.

As can be seen from Table 3.3, the Soviet Union tended to repeat its choice of strategy for the importers of the Middle East and the Persian Gulf more regularly than did the United States. The Soviets, for example, never exported to Israel, Jordan, and Saudi Arabia, but the United States delivered weapons at one time or another to each of the nine importers, ranging from the maximum of twenty-six years for Iran to the one year for Syria. Similar patterns are also evident for the other two sets of strategies, and although the differences

Table 3.3 Exporter's Selection of Export, Increase Export, and Export High Strategies, 1951–1976: The Middle East, Persian Gulf, and South Asia[a]

| | Arms Strategies and Exporter | | | | | |
| | Export | | Increase Exports | | Export High | |
Region/Importer	USA	USSR	USA	USSR	USA	USSR
Middle East						
Egypt	5	21	4	14	5	14
Israel	24	0	12	0	10	0
Jordan	16	0	9	0	8	0
Lebanon	7	1	4	1	7	1
Syria	1	21	1	12	1	10
Persian Gulf						
Iran	26	2	15	1	14	2
Iraq	4	19	1	11	1	11
Kuwait	3	1	3	1	3	1
Saudi Arabia	20	0	11	0	12	0
South Asia						
Afghanistan	0	16	0	11	0	11
India	11	18	7	11	7	12
Nepal	0	1	0	1	0	1
Pakistan	19	4	11	2	10	2
Sri Lanka	5	2	3	2	5	2

[a]Cell entries are the number of years that the USA and USSR chose the export, increase exports, and export high strategies for each importer during the 1951–1976 period.

between the exporters on this matter are not especially great, they are probably still responsible for the larger Soviet proportions for both the Middle East and the Persian Gulf. This is because it is generally easier to predict strategies that remain the same from one year to the next. The starred proportions for the United States and that region were slightly larger than those for the Soviet Union, but then it was the Soviet Union's strategies for the importers of South Asia that changed most often.

Although there appear to be no appreciable differences among the proportions for the two exporters, any firm conclusion on this matter must await the results of the statistical tests. These will be performed after the findings on the three naive models have been presented. The same caution also applies to any discussion of the differences among the proportions for the three arms dichotomies. The figures reported in Table 3.2 indicate, for example, that the theoretical model functions best for both exporters in all three regions when the arms dichotomy is export/no export. They also reveal that the proportions for the high/low dichotomy are generally better than those for the increase/decrease strategies. Are these findings likely to be significant? Perhaps not: as with both the time period options and the exporters, the differences among the proportions for the arms dichotomies are not very large. Indeed, they are usually much smaller than the largest difference observed in the table—the .862 obtained for the export/no export strategies of the United States and the Middle East as against the .712 registered for the increase/decrease dichotomy of the same combination of exporter and region. The suspicion, then, is that it may not be altogether appropriate to rank the arms dichotomies on the basis of the figures presented in Table 3.2.

But why are the proportions for the export/no export dichotomy always the best? The answer to this question is rooted in both the quantitative and qualitative deficiencies associated with the arms trade data, as well as in the preceding argument surrounding the differences between the exporters. It is, first of all, much easier to determine whether a country will export arms than it is to be specific about the numbers (or dollar values) of weapons delivered. This second under-taking occupies both the increase/decrease and high/low options, and it necessitates reasonably precise information about weapons transfers. Unfortunately, however, the arms trade data are not regarded as precise, meaning that errors would occur in the designation of the increase/decrease and high/low outcomes. Those errors would probably reduce the accuracy of the predictions for the second and third dichotomies, and that implies comparatively better figures for the export/no export strategies.

Beyond the probable quantitative limitations of the dollar value data is their complete inutility for evaluating the qualitative aspects of the arms trade phenomenon. Weapons transfers can either increase or decrease, for example, in terms of both quantity or quality, but only the first characteristic can be canvassed with the data used in this analysis. The same problem accompanies the application of the data to the high/low dichotomy; so, in general, this qualitative deficiency would be expected to have a deleterious effect on the performance of the model for both pairs of strategies. The export/no export dichotomy, on the other hand, is not constrained in this fashion because it circumvents the qualitative issue. Overall, then, the dollar value data are perhaps less sensitive, both quantitatively and qualitatively, than they ought to be for measuring the increase/decrease and high/low strategies, and this probably contributes to the slightly larger proportions for the export/no export dichotomy.

The third reason for the larger export/no export proportions revolves around the frequency with which certain strategies are selected. This factor seemed to have an impact on the differences between the exporters: the best exporter-to-region proportions were always associated with the country whose strategies remained the same over time. The same pattern now emerges for the arms dichotomies: the proportions for the export/no export dichotomy are consistently the largest, but then, too, an optimal policy chosen under that dichotomy tends to be reselected with greater regularity than the optimal policies for the other two sets of strategies. This condition holds for both the United States and the Soviet Union and for each of the first three regions. Consider once more the information in Table 3.3. There are a number of countries listed in that table that often received weapons from either the United States or the Soviet Union. The twenty-six years over which the United States exported arms to Iran certainly stand out, but even some of the lesser totals—down perhaps to the eighteen years for the Soviet Union and India—are also indicative of fairly constant arms export relationships. Then there are the figures for the increase export and export high options. The totals for the United States and Iran on these strategies are fifteen and fourteen respectively, and the entries for all of the other dyads in which arms were exported on more than eighteen occasions range from ten to fourteen. In short, countries that normally received arms from either the United States or the Soviet Union saw their weapons shipments decrease about as often as they increased, and they were given high export totals no more frequently than low ones. The arms trade choices of the superpowers were, therefore, much less consistent under the second and third dichotomies than they were under the first, and this distinction probably also contributes to the slightly larger export/no export proportions.

If this last argument is correct, then the proportions for the increase/decrease and high/low dichotomies of the afore-mentioned dyads should be the smallest. Table 3.4 presents the exporter-to-importer proportions covering all possible combinations of dyads and arms dichotomies. The figures reported in the table coincide with the starred exporter-to-region proportions of Table 3.2. Of course, for a few exporter and arms dichotomy combinations, starred proportions were simultaneously registered for both the first and second time period options. The exporter-to-importer results correspond-ing to either of these two time periods could be included in Table 3.4, but only the results for option 1 are presented. This choice is entirely arbitrary and carries no special signifi-cance beyond the fact that all subsequent analyses involving those particular exporter and arms dichotomy combinations will also center on the findings for option 1.

All expectations concerning the performance of the theoretical model for certain dyads and dichotomies are borne out by the proportions in Table 3.4. The figures down the first column demonstrate that the model functions very well for virtually every importer when the arms dichotomy is export/no export. The smallest proportion is .654 (obtained for both the United States and Lebanon and the United States and Saudi Arabia), but even that value indicates that the model is capable of predicting the correct strategy about two-thirds of the time. Of course, the proportions for the other two dichotomies are much smaller and, as anticipated, the steepest reductions

Table 3.4 Proportion of Correct Predictions for Theoretical Model (Exporter-to-Importer): The Middle East, the Persian Gulf, and South Asia

		Export/No Export			Increase/Decrease			High/Low		
			N	Time[a]		N	Time[a]		N	Time[a]
Middle East Dyad										
USA	Egypt	.923			.880			.917		
	Israel	.962			.480			.625		
	Jordan	.808			.600			.667		
	Lebanon	.654			.640			.625		
	Syria	.962	26	$t1$	.960	25	$t2$	.958	24	$t2$
USSR	Egypt	.885			.480			.583		
	Israel	.962			1.000			1.000		
	Jordan	.923			.920			.917		
	Lebanon	.846			.840			.833		
	Syria	.846	26	$t1$	.600	25	$t2$	.542	24	$t2$
Persian Gulf Dyad										
USA	Iran	.885			.680			.750		
	Iraq	.923			.880			.875		
	Kuwait	.846			.880			.875		
	Saudi Arabia	.654	26	$t1$	.560	25	$t1$	.708	24	$t1$
USSR	Iran	.808			.792			.792		
	Iraq	.808			.708			.708		
	Kuwait	1.000			.958			.917		
	Saudi Arabia	.962	26	$t2$	.874	24	$t3$	.917	24	$t1$
South Asia Dyad										
USA	Afghanistan	.923			.960			.917		
	India	.769			.680			.708		
	Nepal	.923			.840			.875		
	Pakistan	.808			.640			.667		
	Sri Lanka	.846	26	$t1$	.760	25	$t2$	.750	24	$t2$
USSR	Afghanistan	.769			.542			.750		
	India	.808			.583			.625		
	Nepal	.885			.833			.833		
	Pakistan	.885			.833			.875		
	Sri Lanka	.808	26	$t2$	.833	24	$t3$	.833	24	$t2$

[a] The N and time period option for each combination of exporter and arms dichotomy apply to all of the importers in a region.

are for the dyads that show the exporter delivering weapons on a fairly regular basis, but which also reveal that the exporter would not settle on particular strategies from either the increase/decrease or high/low options. Such dyads surface in all three regions, but those of the Middle East yield the poorest results. The proportions for the increase/decrease and high/low strategies of the United States and Israel, the Soviet Union and Egypt, and the Soviet Union and Syria range from .480 to .625, and these, quite frankly, are not the kinds of scores that inspire much trust in the ability of the model to capture the decisionmaking for the most meaningful cases.

Although the results for the specially selected Middle East dyads are a disappointment, their impact is eased somewhat by the findings on the comparable dyads of the Persian Gulf and South Asia. The increase/decrease and high/low proportions for the United States and Iran, the United States and Saudi Arabia, and the Soviet Union and Iraq are usually above the .700 mark, and there is only one figure—the .560 for the United States and Saudi Arabia and the increase/decrease dichotomy —that can be characterized as unacceptable. Especially gratifying are the findings for the three Persian Gulf dyads and the high/low option. The proportions for the United States and Saudi Arabia as well as for the Soviet Union and Iraq are each .708, while the entry for the United States and Iran is a lofty .750. The scores for some of the South Asian dyads (i.e., for the United States and both India and Pakistan, as well as for the Soviet Union and both Afghanistan and India) are not quite up to the standards of the gulf, but most are better than the .625 upper value obtained for the special cases of the Middle East. In conclusion, apart from a few unsavory findings (most of which occurred for the Middle East), superpower arms strategies that fluctuate over time are predicted moderately well by the theoretical model (especially for the Persian Gulf and South Asia), and this generally upbeat assessment is complemented by the larger proportions obtained for most other dyads.

The final theoretical model analysis focuses on the four expected-utility submodels. Table 3.5 presents the exporter-to-region proportions for all possible combinations of submodels, exporters, regions, and arms dichotomies. The proportions are simply a breakdown into submodels of the starred theoretical model proportions of Table 3.2. The table also presents for each combination of exporter and arms dichotomy a proportion that summarizes the performance of each submodel over the first three regions. Some of these summary proportions—specifically, those for the noncompetitive-cooperative and noncompetitive-conflictual submodels—will be revised once the results for Central America are incorporated into the discussion. Any permanent judgments regarding the submodels must, therefore, be postponed until the end of the next section.

Table 3.5 Proportion of Correct Predictions for Each Submodel of Theoretical Model (Exporter-to-Region): The Middle East, the Persian Gulf, and South Asia

Submodel	Region	Export/No Export USA	N	USSR	N	Arms Strategies and Exporters Increase/Decrease USA	N	USSR	N	High/Low USA	N	USSR	N
Noncompetitive-Cooperative	ME	---	0	---	0	---	0	---	0	---	0	---	0
	PG	.667	9	1.000	9	.714	7	1.000	5	.600	5	1.000	5
	SA	.875	8	1.000	8	.714	7	.800	5	.800	10	1.000	5
	Sum.	.765	17	1.000	17	.714	14	.900	10	.700	15	1.000	10
Noncompetitive-Conflictual	ME	.840	25	.840	25	.700	20	.800	20	.667	15	.733	15
	PG	1.000	11	1.000	11	.889	9	.857	7	.858	7	.858	7
	SA	.917	12	.833	12	.750	8	.800	5	.600	5	1.000	5
	Sum.	.896	48	.875	48	.757	37	.813	32	.703	27	.815	27
Competitive-Cooperative	ME	---	0	---	0	---	0	---	0	---	0	---	0
	PG	.800	45	.867	45	.711	45	.800	45	.756	45	.844	45
	SA	.869	46	.826	46	.848	46	.739	46	.826	46	.826	46
	Sum.	.835	91	.846	91	.780	91	.769	91	.791	91	.835	91
Competitive-Conflictual	ME	.867	105	.905	105	.714	105	.762	105	.771	105	.781	105
	PG	.846	39	.872	39	.769	39	.846	39	.872	39	.795	39
	SA	.828	64	.813	64	.734	64	.703	64	.765	64	.719	64
	Sum.	.851	208	.870	208	.731	208	.760	208	.788	208	.764	208

Note: ME is Middle East; PG is Persian Gulf; SA is South Asia.

The information contained in Table 3.5 conforms with almost everything else that has been discovered about the theoretical model. Consistency has been the hallmark of the results; it has been registered across the proportions for the time period options, the exporters, the arms dichotomies, and the first three regions. And there is nothing at all that emanates from Table 3.5 that challenges the remarkable degree of consistency that has been found thus far. There are, naturally, some variations over the entries for the submodels just as there were differences among the proportions for the time period options, the exporters, and so on. But, like those other differences, the ones that surface over the figures in Table 3.5 are simply not compelling. The truly striking feature is that every single summary proportion—and there are twenty-four of them—is at or above the .700 mark, meaning that each of the four expected-utility models is performing reasonably well. Of course, the proportions for the first two submodels are based on a relatively small number of cases. Moreover, those scores will undoubtedly decline as the dismal findings for the United States and Central America become a part of the tabulations. Yet, even with these caveats, the results presented in Table 3.5, together with all of the other findings on the theoretical model, still suggest the tentative conclusion that arms trade policymaking has been properly conceived for the first three regions. In particular, it seems to be a process that can be modeled by expected-utility theory. That means that the process can be approached probabilistically, that rationality can be ascribed to the behavior patterns of the actors, and that utility-maximization can be posited as the decisionmaking standard.

It seems also to be a process that is virtually identical for the United States and the Soviet Union. Whether the two countries are contemplating the export/no export, increase/ decrease, or high/low strategies, whether they are evaluating those options for importers of the Middle East, the Persian Gulf, or South Asia, the results are almost always the same. What is found for one exporter is also found for the other, and, more often than not, the findings speak well of the theoretical model. Now, to all of this is added one further observation. The data in Table 3.5 indicate not only that expected-utility theory is relevant to arms trade decisionmaking, but also that the practice of partitioning the decisionmaking process into several subprocesses to take into account particular environmental conditions probably has some theoretical merit. Had the policymaking been the same for all four environments (i.e., had there been only one policymaking process), then perhaps just one of the submodels would have been able to capture it, such that the proportions obtained for that submodel would have been considerably larger than those obtained for the others. Inasmuch as there are no sizable differences among the proportions for the submodels, the possibility exists that the superpowers were inclined to adjust their decisionmaking to fit the circumstances of particular environments. Of course, this is just a tentative interpretation that applies only to the decisionmaking for the Middle East, the Persian Gulf, and South Asia. Its merits will be evaluated further in the next section on Central America.

Central America

The results for the United States and Central America reported in Table 3.2 seem to contravene many of the findings for the first three regions. Time period options 1 and 2 (especially the latter), for example, were identified previously as the best predictors of superpower export policies; however, for Central America, time period option 3 performs almost as well as option 1, while option 2 emerges as the least effective. The findings for the three sets of arms strategies are no less contradictory. The largest proportions for the past three regions were consistently obtained for the export/no export strategies, but the largest proportions for this fourth region correspond to the high/low alternatives. The figures for the export/no export strategies are even slightly smaller than those for the increase/decrease options. The only favorable Central American outcome happens also to be a contradiction. The proportions for the Soviet Union are much better than those for the United States, but this is inconsistent with the earlier discovery of essentially identical superpower arms trade patterns.

The other theoretical model findings should probably be presented before speculating about the reasons for the unusual results. The first of these are the exporter-to-importer proportions corresponding to the exporter-to-region figures of

Table 3.2. This information is reported in Table 3.6. The proportions for the United States in Table 3.6 are simply a breakdown into dyads of the starred proportions in the earlier table. The scores for the Soviet Union correspond to any of the best time period options relating to each arms dichotomy in Table 3.2. This is possible because each of the starred exporter-to-region proportions in Table 3.2 yields the same exporter-to-importer scores. The figures for the Soviet Union are only reported for the sake of consistency.

The proportions in Table 3.6 are generally no better than those of Table 3.2. The findings for the Soviet Union are certainly satisfactory, but they are also of little consequence because that country never once delivered weapons to any of the Central American states during the 1951–1976 period. Among the proportions obtained for the United States, only those for Nicaragua are palatable. The .760 registered for the export/no export dichotomy is perhaps the most encouraging of these because, if the model had consistently predicted the no export strategy (the strategy that the United States chose most often for Nicaragua), the proportion would have been .640. Still, the difference between .760 and .640 is not particularly great, which means that if there is to be relief for Central America, it must emerge from the differences between the

Table 3.6 Proportion of Correct Predictions for Theoretical Model (Exporter-to-Importer): Central America

| | | Export/No Export | | Increase/Decrease | | High/Low | | |
		N	Time	N	Time	N	Time
Central America Dyad								
USA	Costa Rica	.480		.458		.542		
	El Salvador	.600		.583		.583		
	Guatemala	.520		.542		.542		
	Honduras	.320		.458		.667		
	Nicaragua	.760		.667		.750		
	Panama	.520	25	t3	.542	24	t3	.625	24	t1
USSR	Costa Rica	.885		.880		.875		
	El Salvador	.923		.920		.917		
	Guatemala	1.000		1.000		1.000		
	Honduras	1.000		1.000		1.000		
	Nicaragua	1.000		1.000		1.000		
	Panama	1.000	26	t1/t2	1.000	25	t1/t2	1.000	24	t1/t2

Above the sub-headers: Arms Strategies[a]

[a]The N and time period option for each combination of exporter and arms dichotomy apply to all six importers.

Table 3.7 Proportion of Correct Predictions for Each Submodel of Theoretical Model (Exporter-to-Region): Central America

Submodel	USA	N	USSR	N	USA	N	USSR	N	USA	N	USSR	N
							Arms Strategies and Exporters					
Noncompetitive-Cooperative	.496	113	.975	119	.485	107	.973	113	.579	107	.972	107
Noncompetitive-Conflictual	.659	37	.946	37	.702	37	.946	37	.730	37	.946	37
Competitive-Cooperative	---	0	---	0	---	0	---	0	---	0	---	0
Competitive-Conflictual	---	0	---	0	---	0	---	0	---	0	---	0

proportions for the noncompetitive-cooperative and noncompetitive-conflictual submodels. These proportions are presented in Table 3.7.

The information reported in Table 3.7 may be the most significant of all of the findings that have been presented. The key figures are for the United States, located in columns one, three, and five. They show that the submodel for the noncompetitive-conflictual environment functions much better than the submodel for the noncompetitive-cooperative. The entries for the noncompetitive-conflictual submodel may not be as good as the scores obtained for the submodels of the other regions, but they are respectable, especially when contrasted with the proportions for the noncompetitive-cooperative submodel. Of course, the noncompetitive-cooperative submodel has been used for most of the Central American cases (compare the Ns between rows one and two); hence, that submodel must be responsible for the unsavory findings in Tables 3.2 and 3.6. The proportions in those tables probably would have been better if Central America had been noncompetitive-conflictual more often.

Why does the submodel for the noncompetitive-cooperative environment operate so poorly? One conceivable explanation focuses on the characteristics of importers that reside within that kind of environment. Countries that seek or accept military assistance in the absence of an immediate foreign threat (which is, by definition, one of the characteristics of noncompetitive-cooperative importers) probably do so in order to suppress or otherwise forestall internal opposition. This concern would have been particularly urgent for the Central American states, most of which were governed by unpopular and precarious military dictatorships for much of the 1951–1976 period. It also happens to be just one of the many factors that fall within the rubric of importer motivations; it is a part of what Frank called the "demand factors" of the arms trade environment. As a demand factor, the inclination to acquire arms for purposes of maintaining internal security might obviously apply to any of the four decisionmaking settings; it need not be peculiar to the noncompetitive-cooperative environment. Nonetheless, its omission may be felt more for that environment because, while the general theoretical model is never very attentive to the issues that concern importing countries, it is particularly negligent under conditions noncompetitive-cooperative decision-making. The deliberative process for that environment is only represented by lotteries that deal with the exporter's own relations. The processes for the other three environments, however, include lotteries that attend to subjects (regional competition and regional relations) that are at least tangentially related to the kinds of evaluations conducted by importers. These additional lotteries may be able to compensate for the model's general disregard of demand factors in the other environments, but no such redemptive provision exists for the noncompetitive-cooperative setting.

The specific demand factor discussed here—the issue of internal security—seems even more compelling when it is remembered that the only country for which the predictions of the United States were satisfactory happened also to be the country that had the most external conflict. Nicaragua was constantly experiencing border problems throughout the 1951–1976 era (first with Costa Rica and then with Honduras), and this is reflected by the fact that its environment was noncompetitive-conflictual more often than the environments of the other Central American states. This is not to say, of course, that Nicaragua's Somoza governments were unconcerned about matters of internal security. That is unlikely. Instead, it simply suggests that the foreign policy constraints faced by those governments (especially with regard to regional relations) were probably sufficiently prominent for the model to pick up. The other Central American importers, on the other hand, experienced fewer instances of foreign conflict, and the predictions for the United States and those countries were much less accurate. Again, the reason for this may be the existence of actuating domestic political demand factors that the model simply does not consider.

Of course, the small proportions for the dyads involving the United States may instead be due to the usual difficulty of predicting strategies that change over time. Table 3.8—the Central American counterpart to Table 3.3—demonstrates that the United States often shifted between the export and no export strategies for El Salvador, Guatemala, Honduras, and Nicaragua. This factor probably contributes to the poor predictions, but it is worth remembering that the results for similar dyads of both the Persian Gulf and South Asia were relatively good, and that overall they have never been as unfavorable as they are now for Central America. There is also the problem of Costa Rica, a country to which the United States never exported weapons. On the basis of the pattern established for the previous regions, the proportions for that dyad should be among the best, yet they are actually the worst (see Table 3.6). The extraordinary characteristics of the Costa Rican internal scene—as evidenced by that country's lack of a military establishment—may very well account for the discrepancy.

The only remaining issue concerning the theoretical model is the overall performances of the four submodels. Table 3.9 presents the proportion of correct exporter-to-region predictions for each combination of submodel and arms dichotomy. The table summarizes (by combining and

Table 3.8 Exporter's Selection of Export, Increase Exports, and Export High Strategies, 1951–1976: Central America[a]

Central America Importer	Export	U.S. Strategies Increase Exports	Export High
Costa Rica	0	0	0
El Salvador	8	6	7
Guatemala	12	7	5
Honduras	16	7	7
Nicaragua	9	7	6
Panama	5	4	5

[a]Cell entries are the number of years that the U.S. chose the export, increase exports, and export high strategies for each importer during the 1951–1976 period.

Table 3.9 Exporter-to-Region Proportions for Four Submodels of Theoretical Model[a]

	Arms Trade Strategies					
	Export/No Export	N	Increase/Decrease	N	High/Low	N
Noncompetitive-Cooperative	.585	147	.542	131	.622	127
Noncompetitive-Conflictual	.820	133	.755	106	.747	91
Competitive-Cooperative	.841	182	.775	182	.813	182
Competitive-Conflictual	.861	416	.745	416	.776	416

[a]The figures in the table cover both the United States and the Soviet Union for the Middle East, the Persian Gulf, and South Asia; and the United States for Central America.

recomputing) the submodel findings that were reported for all four regions. The entries in the table generally cover both exporters; however, the noncompetitive-cooperative and noncompetitive-conflictual proportions are not based on any of the predictions involving the Soviet Union and Central America. That information has been excluded so as to avoid distorting the results.

The figures presented in Table 3.9 indicate that three of the four expected-utility submodels function very well. What this means, however, is open to speculation. Nothing conclusive can be said about the submodels without complementary sets of predictions that ignore the differences between decision-making subprocesses. In the absence of these additional analyses, only the most conditional assessment is appropriate: *if* it is indeed the case that hegemonic exporters adjust their decisionmaking over various arms import environments, then it *appears* as though this study has produced expected-utility submodels that represent the decisionmaking for three such environments. Those submodels are the noncompetitive-conflictual, competitive-cooperative, and competitive-conflictual, and the above statement is qualified because of the possibility that one submodel (say, the noncompetitive-conflictual) can yield results that are as good for another environment (say, the competitive-cooperative) as those of the submodel for that environment. If this kind of pattern were to occur regularly—that is, if the various submodels predict as accurately for other environments as they do for their own—there would not be any meaningful differences among the environments, and the overall achievement would be the discovery of three expected-utility *models* that are equally adept at capturing the policymaking process.

Of course, this scenario is also speculation, and not a very convincing script at that. There is nothing that indicates that the initial decision to partition the policymaking process into four subprocesses was unnecessary. Indeed, given the rather pronounced differences between the submodels (as is indicated by the lotteries assigned to each), it is unlikely that all would produce the same outcomes were they to be administered indiscriminately over the various environments. Nor can it be said that one particular lottery is the key to obtaining good results. The poor performance of the noncompetitive-cooperative submodel demonstrates, for example, that Lotteries 1 and 2 cannot exclusively account for the larger proportions in the table. By the same token, it cannot be argued that either Lottery 3 or 4 is singularly responsible for the better findings for the simple reason that each is excluded from one of three submodels that perform well. In short, the notion of distinct policymaking subprocesses remains eminently plausible, and that suggests a deeper meaning to the results. The interpretation preferred here is that the expected-utility model is especially well suited to describing the decisionmaking for Third World regions that are unstable. The instability may be in the form of an intractable interstate dispute, or it may be seen in the competition between hegemonic powers for friends and clients. Whatever its manifestation, the model always functions better when there is at least some instability present, but it performs poorly when a Third World region is both competition-free and pacific. These last two characteristics distinguish the noncompetitive-cooperative setting, and arms transfer arrangements for countries in such regions seem less a function of the issues that interest hegemonic exporters (competition, regional conflict) and more a result of the factors that concern importers (internal security, prestige, and so on). This is the demand side of the arms trade phenomenon, a perspective that is simply not entertained by the expected-utility model.

This interpretation also clarifies the substantial differences between the findings for Central America and the other regions. The expected-utility model operates best for the Middle East, the Persian Gulf, and South Asia because those three regions were the most unstable during the 1951–1976 period. Wars between the Arabs and the Israelis, between India and Pakistan, together with numerous small-scale disputes and the incessant rivalry between the superpowers, all created the conditions upon which the expected-utility model apparently thrives. Central America, on the other hand, was noticeably different. The region certainly had its share of conflicts, but they were not as persistent or as intense as the confrontations that surfaced in the first three regions. Nor were they supplemented by any sort of superpower competition. In short, the Central American environment was comparatively stable, a circumstance that is not consistent with the strengths of the expected-utility model. Thus, it is for this reason that the poorest results are those for Central America.

Naive Models and Statistical Tests

The purpose of this section is to compare the findings for the theoretical model with the results for naive models 1, 2, and 3, and then to administer the analysis of variance and Tukey statistical tests to determine whether any differences between models, exporters, and arms dichotomies are statistically significant. The three naive models entertained in this analysis are simplifications of the theoretical model. Naive model 1 disposes of the w_j nation weight, proposing instead that an exporter would be disinclined to make any judgments concerning the relative importance of the countries in the import region as it determines its arms trade strategy for the prospective importer. Naive model 2 eliminates the need for country-by-country estimates of the political relations variables (i.e., the c variables) as it assigns to each of those variables the value of the one boundary that is assumed to express the exporter's actual attitude toward the political relations outcome of the associated utility. Finally, naive model 3 combines the amendments of the first and second naive models by dropping the w_j nation weight and by specifying boundary values for the political relations variables.

These three models have also been used to predict Soviet and U.S. arms trade strategies for the importers of the four regions, and Table 3.10 presents the exporter-to-region proportions relating to those predictions. The proportions correspond to the time period options that were found to be the best predictors for the theoretical model, and the table also includes the figures for the theoretical model (from Table 3.2) to facilitate the task of comparing all four models. The Ns reported in the rightmost column of the table apply to each cell in a row.

The four models are arranged in Table 3.10 according to their anticipated capabilities. The largest proportions should be obtained for the theoretical model (TM) followed, in order, by the proportions for naive models 1 (N1) through 3 (N3). Naive model 1 is expected to be more accurate than naive model 2 because deleting w_j amounts to a less extensive

Table 3.10 Proportion of Correct Predictions for Theoretical and Naive Models (Exporter-to-Region)

Region/ Exporter	Arms Strategies	TM	N1	N2	N3	Time	N^a
				Model			
Middle East							
USA	Export/No Export	.862	.846	.815	.385	t1	130
	Increase/Decrease	.712	.696	.648	.472	t2	125
	High/Low	.758	.742	.667	.450	t2	120
USSR	Export/No Export	.892	.792	.538	.354	t1	130
	Increase/Decrease	.768	.720	.536	.464	t2	125
	High/Low	.775	.708	.525	.425	t2	120
Persian Gulf							
USA	Export/No Export	.827	.798	.683	.558	t1	104
	Increase/Decrease	.750	.730	.620	.650	t1	100
	High/Low	.802	.771	.688	.615	t1	96
USSR	Export/No Export	.894	.721	.779	.615	t2	104
	Increase/Decrease	.833	.688	.771	.656	t3	96
	High/Low	.833	.792	.729	.635	t1	96
South Asia							
USA	Export/No Export	.854	.785	.669	.446	t1	130
	Increase/Decrease	.776	.704	.704	.512	t2	125
	High/Low	.783	.675	.692	.483	t2	120
USSR	Export/No Export	.831	.754	.615	.585	t2	130
	Increase/Decrease	.725	.658	.617	.617	t3	120
	High/Low	.783	.733	.667	.617	t2	120
Central America							
USA	Export/No Export	.533	.533	.500	.493	.t3	150
	Increase/Decrease	.542	.542	.486	.479	t3	144
	High/Low	.618	.632	.576	.563	t1	144
USSR	Export/No Export	.968	.949	.962	.936	t1 or t2	156
	Increase/Decrease	.967	.947	.960	.933	t1 or t2	150
	High/Low	.965	.944	.958	.931	t1 or t2	144

^{a}The N in each row applies to each proportion within the row.

revision of the theoretical model than modifying all of the political relations variables. When the features of the first and second naive models are combined, however, as in naive model 3, predictive accuracy should be reduced even further. The figures presented in Table 3.10 for the Middle East, the Persian Gulf, and South Asia generally conform to these expectations. The proportions almost always become progressively smaller from the theoretical model to naive model 3, and this is evident for both the United States and the Soviet Union and for all three arms dichotomies. The same pattern is also exhibited for the United States and Central America, although, for that exporter and region, the drop in predictive accuracy is much less precipitous than the declines witnessed for the first three regions.

Of course, these are just general observations. Exceptions can be detected throughout the table, and some of the findings deserve more concentrated attention. Of particular interest, for example, are the proportions for the theoretical model. These are consistently larger than the proportions obtained for any of the other models over each of the first three regions, confirming that the theoretical model is the truest representation of the policymaking process. Notice, however, that the differences between the proportions for the theoretical model and naive model 1 are not especially large. The steepest declines are for the Soviet Union and the Persian Gulf, but these are easily offset by a number of other comparisons that reveal only minor differences between the two models. All of this obviously suggests that the theoretical model will not always be significantly better than naive model 1. It may indeed be the most effective model developed in this study, but its advantages are probably not sizable enough to warrant recommending it over all of the other models under every circumstance.

Whatever the findings for the theoretical model and naive model 1, virtually all of the test outcomes concerning the models should reveal statistically significant differences. This applies to the across the board reductions from the theoretical model to naive model 3, as well as to the remaining pairwise comparisons between models. Of course, these expectations only cover the proportions for the first three regions. The test results for Central America should be substantially different. In fact, there are no positive expectations connected with the findings for that region. All four models perform poorly, and the only really noticeable distinction—that between the two exporters—is completely meaningless. All of this means, then, that Central America must once again be characterized as a deviant case. Any hope that the naive models would be better suited to the features of the noncompetitive-cooperative import environment has been dashed by the figures in Table 3.10. Statistical tests will still be performed on the predictions for the region, but the principal purpose for these is to ensure that the findings for Central America are analyzed in the same manner as those for the other regions.

In addition to evaluating the differences between the theoretical and naive models, the statistical tests to be performed in this section also search for significant differences between the two exporters and the three arms dichotomies. These latter two issues were given some consideration during the presentation of the results for the theoretical model, and the conclusion then was that the differences between the exporters and the arms dichotomies were probably too meager to warrant any substantial rethinking of the policymaking process. The initial thesis of virtually identical Soviet and U.S. decisionmaking procedures seemed entirely justified, and there was also ample support for the proposition that these procedures would remain the same for each of the three pairs of strategies the two exporters might contemplate. These two statements number among the more important theoretical contributions of this study, and the information presented on the naive models scarcely challenges their validity. Each naive model performs about as well for one exporter as it does for the other, and each is similarly proficient for the three arms dichotomies. The one major exception to either of these conclusions concerns the Middle East and naive model 2, where the proportion for the United States and the export/no export dichotomy (.815) is considerably larger than the corresponding entry for the Soviet Union (.538). This is a peculiar finding, which could be viewed as evidence of two entirely different policymaking processes; however, that interpretation would be much too radical. The gap between the exporters disappears with the export/no export proportions for naive model 3, and most of the other differences between the two countries are much smaller. In short, the preponderance of the evidence clearly indicates that, while there may be significant differences among the theoretical and naive models, no such differences ought to be anticipated for either the arms dichotomies or the exporters.

This discussion once again emphasizes the tremendous correspondence across the results for the first three regions. In general, what is found for the Middle East is also found for the Persian Gulf and South Asia. Yet, beneath this broad pattern of consistency are the decidedly uneven results for naive model 3. The proportions for that model range from .354 to .472 for the Middle East, .446 to .617 for South Asia, and .558 to .656

for the Persian Gulf. These differences suggest that both w_j and empirically derived values for the political relations variables are more important for the Middle East than they are for either the Persian Gulf or South Asia. Why would this be the case? One conceivable explanation emerges from the environmental records of the three regions. The Middle East was always conflictual and usually competitive, and the relationships between the countries in that region, as well as between those states and the superpowers, were unambiguous and enduring. The w_j nation weights and empirical estimates of the political relations variables may be of greater consequence for that kind of region because they can easily detect the nations that are important to the superpowers, and emphasize friendships and hostilities among all of the countries. Dabbling with those variables (as through naive model 3) reduces their effectiveness, and that may be why the Middle East proportions for naive model 3 are as small as they are.

The same adjustments are not as debilitating, however, for either the Persian Gulf or South Asia, and the reason for this may be the murkey political atmospheres surrounding those regions. Iraq's relations with Iran, Kuwait, and Saudi Arabia seemed to alternate between periods of conflict and cooperation, and fluctuations could also be detected in the relationship between some of the gulf states and the superpowers. Similar conditions also surfaced in South Asia. The United States, for example, endured highs and lows in its relations with both Pakistan and India, and the Soviet Union had comparable experiences with Pakistan. These political relations fluctuations diminish the utility of both w_j and the c variable estimates, meaning that the consequences of eliminating or simplifying them would be much less severe for the Persian Gulf and South Asia than they were for the Middle East. The proportions for naive model 3 are completely consistent with this argument. They may be smaller for South Asia than they are for the Persian Gulf, but then, too, the South Asian internal scene was also more predictable. Relations between India and Pakistan, between India and China, and between Pakistan and Afghanistan scarcely budged from their conflictual patterns. At the same time, all other South Asian relationships generally remained cooperative. There was, then, enough consistency embodied in the political relationships of the South Asian states to make the c variable estimates more decisive and the proportions for South Asia smaller than those for the Persian Gulf.

The differences across the first three regions on naive model 3 are not so profound as to alter expectations concerning the statistical tests. The initial test is a three-way analysis of variance with the *proportion of correct predictions* as the criterion variable, and *model, exporter,* and *arms dichotomy* as the three factors. The test will be administered individually for each of the four regions because of the region-specific nature of the predictions and models. This means that four separate three-way tests will be conducted. The purpose of each of these tests is to determine whether a significant portion of the variation (or total sum of squares) in the proportion of correct predictions is attributable to any of the three factors. The null hypothesis for each factor stipulates that its contribution to the variation will be negligible; however, for the first three regions, the differences between the models are expected to have significant effects, while the differences between the exporters and the arms dichotomies are not. What are anticipated, then, are F ratios that are large enough to reject the null hypotheses for *model,* but other F ratios that are too small to reject for both *exporter* and *arms dichotomy.* The first of these results would not necessarily establish that the theoretical model is a significantly better representation of the arms trade process than the other models; however, given the findings on the first three regions in Table 3.10, it would suggest that progress from naive model 3 to the theoretical model would bring one significantly closer to capturing that process. The other two findings would indicate that the policymaking processes of the United States and the Soviet Union are similar and that the models developed in this study are equally applicable to each of the three conceptualizations of arms transfer strategies.

The data that are needed for the analyses of variance are the exporter-to-importer proportions corresponding to all of the exporter-to-region figures in Table 3.10. This information is located in Tables 3.4 and 3.6 for the theoretical model and in the Appendix for the three naive models. The results of the analyses of variance are presented in Table 3.11. Included in the table are the sum of squares, degrees of freedom (DF), mean square (estimate of the variance), the value of the F statistic, and the significance of F corresponding to the three

Table 3.11 Analysis of Variance

Criterion Variable: Proportion of Correct Predictions
Factors: Model (MOD), Exporter (EXP), Arms Dichotomy (AD)

Middle East

Sources of Variation	Sum of Squares	DF	Mean Square	F	Significance of F
Main Effects (Joint)	2.647	6	.441	18.135	.001
MOD	2.493	3	.831	34.168	.001
EXP	.066	1	.066	2.713	.103
AD	.087	2	.044	1.796	.171
Two-way Interactions	.394	11	.036	1.474	.154
MOD and EXP	.185	3	.062	2.538	.061
MOD and AD	.184	6	.031	1.261	.283
EXP and AD	.025	2	.013	.516	.598
Three-way Interaction MOD, EXP, AD	.024	6	.004	.165	.986
Residual	2.335	96	.024		
Total	5.400	119	.045		

South Asia

Sources of Variation	Sum of Squares	DF	Mean Square	F	Significance of F
Main Effects (Joint)	1.102	6	.169	8.793	.001
MOD	.993	3	.331	17.257	.001
EXP	.003	1	.003	.152	.698
AD	.016	2	.008	.416	.661
Two-way Interactions	.250	11	.023	1.186	.307
MOD and EXP	.143	3	.048	2.483	.065
MOD and AD	.088	6	.015	.768	.597
EXP and AD	.019	2	.009	.495	.611
Three-way Interaction MOD, EXP, AD	.007	6	.001	.057	.999
Residual	1.841	96	.019		
Total	3.109	119	.026		

Persian Gulf

Sources of Variation	Sum of Squares	DF	Mean Square	F	Significance of F
Main Effects (Joint)	.570	6	.095	3.862	.002
MOD	.522	3	.174	7.079	.001
EXP	.036	1	.036	1.480	.228
AD	.011	2	.006	.227	.798
Two-way Interactions	.103	11	.009	.379	.960
MOD and EXP	.054	3	.018	.733	.536
MOD and AD	.046	6	.008	.313	.928
EXP and AD	.002	2	.001	.047	.954
Three-way Interaction MOD, EXP, AD	.022	6	.004	.151	.988
Residual	1.770	72	.025		
Total	2.465	95	.026		

Central America

Sources of Variation	Sum of Squares	DF	Mean Square	F	Significance of F
Main Effects (Joint)	6.149	6	1.025	179.556	.001
MOD	.040	3	.013	2.319	.079
EXP	6.057	1	6.057	1061.222	.001
AD	.052	2	.026	4.577	.012
Two-way Interactions	.080	11	.007	1.276	.246
MOD and EXP	.019	3	.006	1.098	.353
MOD and AD	.001	6	.000	.034	.999
EXP and AD	.060	2	.030	5.269	.006
Three-way Interaction MOD, EXP, AD	.001	6	.000	.031	.999
Residual	.685	120	.006		
Total	6.915	143	.048		

factors and to all two-way and three-way interaction effects. The table also reports the total sum of squares, or the total variation in the criterion variable, and the residual sum of squares, or that portion of the total variation that is not attributable to any of the three factors.

The effects of the three factors for each of the first three regions is believed to be additive rather than interactive. This means, for example, that the differences between the models should produce the same effect on the proportion of correct predictions regardless of the exporter, and, likewise, that the differences between the exporters should produce the same effect on the proportion of correct predictions regardless of the model. In other words, if each factor is to make a significant contribution to the total variation, then it will do so independently of the other factors. The implication of this additivity assumption is that the sum of squares attributable to each two-way and three-way interaction should not be significant. The F ratios reported in Table 3.11 support this contention; not one of the two-way or three-way interactions is significant at the .05 level for any of the first three regions.

Additivity in the four analyses of variance models is relayed by the main, or independent, effects of the three factors. The first of these main effects is the joint effect, or that portion of the total variation that is due to the individual effects of all three factors. Table 3.11 reveals that the sums of squares for the joint effects of the first three regions generate F ratios that are significant at either the .001 or .002 level. The implication of these significant joint effects is that at least one of the other main effects for the same regions must also be significant. The F ratios obtained for *exporter* and *arms dichotomy* never are, at least not at the .05 level; however, the F ratios for *model* are significant, and always at the .001 level. The meaning is clear: for the Middle East, the Persian Gulf, and South Asia, the null hypotheses for *model* can be rejected, but the null hypotheses for *exporter* and *arms dichotomy* cannot. The differences between the models are, in fact, responsible for a significant portion of the total variation in the proportion of correct predictions, but the differences between the exporters and the arms dichotomies are not.

Of course, the test outcomes for Central America are completely different. The key result for that region is neither the significant main effect for *arms dichotomy* nor the significant main effect for *exporter*; rather, it is the significance of the two-way interaction between those factors. This finding indicates that, while there may be significant differences among the proportions for the three pairs of arms strategies, those differences are probably due to the extremely large differences that already exist between the proportions for the United States and the Soviet Union. This seems perfectly reasonable. The differences among the proportions in Table 3.10 for the three Central American arms dichotomies are simply not large enough to expect that *arms dichotomy* alone could account for a significant part of the variation. As for the finding on *exporter*, it is best interpreted as the product of two relatively uninspiring conditions: (1) that the model is unable to capture the decisionmaking process of the United States; and (2) that the model is capable of advancing the correct default option when there happens to be *no* Soviet decisionmaking. Neither of these conditions is especially satisfying, yet each has some bearing on the test outcome for *model*. This factor is not statistically significant, which means that all four models are unrepresentative of U.S. decisionmaking even while all are capable of picking the default option for the Soviet Union.

The test results for Central American are not particularly surprising. They merely confirm most everything that has already been determined about the relevance of expected-utility theory for that region. Nor are they overly distressing. What has been found for Central America may not be appealing, but the impact of those findings is eased considerably by the implications of the analyses of variance for the first three regions. Those tests demonstrate that the policy-making processes of the United States and the Soviet Union are virtually identical and that they remain the same for any of the various ways the two exporters define their arms transfer options. They also disclose that significant differences exist among the expected-utility models in terms of their ability to represent the decisionmaking process. All that need be determined now is whether the differences *between* particular models in each of those regions are statistically significant. This task is accomplished through the Tukey test of multiple comparisons. The data needed for the Tukey test are presented in the top half of Table 3.12. These are the mean proportion of correct predictions for each of the four models. The Tukey test focuses on the means of any two models and specifies whether

Table 3.12 Data for Tukey Test of Multiple Comparisons

Mean Proportion of Correct Predictions for Theoretical and Naive Models

	Regions		
	Middle East	Persian Gulf	South Asia
Models			
Theoretical Model	.80	.83	.79
Naive Model 1	.75	.76	.72
Naive Model 2	.62	.72	.66
Naive Model 3	.43	.62	.54
Parameter Values			
Residual Mean Square (RMS)	.024	.025	.009
N	30.	24.	30.
$\hat{\sigma} = \sqrt{RMS/N}$	.0283	.0323	.0252
c	2.616	2.630	2.616
$c \cdot \hat{\sigma}$	.074	.085	.066

the difference between them is statistically significant.

The Tukey method is a confidence interval approach that relies on the studentized range distribution (Neter and Wasserman 1974). The technique stipulates that all pairwise differences between model means must be $\leq c \cdot \hat{\sigma}$ with a family confidence coefficient of $1 - \alpha$, or .95. The constant $c = q(.95; r, n_T - r)/\sqrt{2}$, while $\hat{\sigma} = \sqrt{\text{Residual Mean Square}/N}$ = the estimated standard deviation of the sample of observations. The value of $q(.95; r, n_T - r)$ is obtained directly from the studentized range distribution table. For the Middle East, $r = 4$ for the number of models, and $n_T = 120$ for the total number of exporter-to-importer proportions that were calculated for that region; hence, $q(.95; 4, 116)$ is approximately equal to 3.7. The second half of Table 3.12 presents all of the information needed to estimate both c and $\hat{\sigma}$ for each of the first three regions. The key entries in the table are the actual values of $c \cdot \hat{\sigma}$. If the pairwise difference between the means of any two models in a particular region is greater than the value of $c \cdot \hat{\sigma}$ for that region, the null hypothesis of no significant difference between the means can be rejected.

All of the Tukey test results are presented in Table 3.13. The procedure has been applied to every possible pairwise combination of the four models and, more often than not, the differences between the models are statistically significant. Certainly, the most satisfying comparisons are between the

Table 3.13 Tukey Pairwise Comparisons

| Model Pairs | Regions | | |
	Middle East	Persian Gulf	South Asia
TM–N1	.80 – .75 = .05	.83 – .76 = .07	.79 – .72 = .07[a]
TM–N2	.80 – .62 = .18[a]	.83 – .72 = .11[a]	.79 – .66 = .13[a]
TM–N3	.80 – .43 = .37[a]	.83 – .62 = .21[a]	.79 – .54 = .25[a]
N1–N2	.75 – .62 = .13[a]	.76 – .72 = .04	.72 – .66 = .06
N1–N3	.75 – .43 = .32[a]	.76 – .62 = .14[a]	.72 – .54 = .18[a]
N2–N3	.62 – .43 = .19[a]	.72 – .62 = .10[a]	.66 – .54 = .12[a]

[a]$P < .05$

theoretical model and naive models 2 and 3. The principal distinction between these models centers on the political relations variables of the utility functions; specifically, the second and third naive models operate on the assumption that the values of the political relations variables can be specified intuitively, while the theoretical model valuates those variables empirically.

Inasmuch as all Tukey comparisons between the theoretical model and naive models 2 and 3 are statistically significant, the empirical approach of the theoretical model must obviously be superior. What precisely does this mean? It means, first of all, that the procedures used to measure the political relations variables have practical validity. Something above and beyond what can be provided by intuition is evidently gained by the elementary indices that have been fashioned in this study and by the conflict and cooperation data that are entertained by those indices. The measurement routine, in other words, is collecting genuinely useful information about the policymaking process. Of course, it is also supplying information. It is demonstrating, in particular, that the policy choices of hegemonic exporters are largely functions of ever changing country-by-country evaluations of the political relationships between states. All four models posit that an exporter's arms trade decision will be influenced by interstate relations, but only the theoretical model proposes that an exporter would actually conduct independent political relations evaluations for each of the many actors, and that it would willingly adjust those evaluations at a later date.

This speaks well of hegemonic exporters. Gathering and processing information on the numerous relationships that may be affected by an arms transfer policy is an undertaking of such considerable cost that it could easily be avoided. It is not difficult to visualize an exporter trying to simplify its decision task, perhaps by establishing general guidelines on interstate relations that would make the choice of policy under any circumstance much easier. This is precisely what is proposed through naive models 2 and 3, but it is thoroughly inconsistent with the decisionmaking routine of the theoretical model. That first model stipulates that an exporter would conduct an exhaustive search for political relations data and that it would process that data in a fashion that would lead to the value-maximizing policy. This is rational decisionmaking; ergo, that the theoretical model performs significantly better than either naive models 2 or 3 means that arms trade policymaking as practiced by hegemonic exporters is an eminently rational process.

But just how extensive is the exporter's quest for information? Another component of the utility functions in the theoretical model is the w_j variable, which weighs the countries of the import region according to their importance to the hegemonic exporter. The variable is eliminated from naive model 1, and the differences between that model and the theoretical model are not statistically significant for either the Middle East or the Persian Gulf. This immediately suggests that the nation weights are unimportant to the policymaking process; they provide the exporter with little information beyond what has already been gained from the political relations variables. But this assessment may be too severe. Notice that the difference between the theoretical model and naive model 1 is statistically significant for South Asia, and that significant differences also exist between naive models 2 (which retains w_j) and 3 (which eliminates the variable) for all three regions. These additional findings indicate that the nation weights can be critical under certain circumstances. For some regions, such as South Asia, the relative importance of each country in the import region will have significance all by itself on the exporter's choice of strategy. The exporter will actually take the time during the course of its decisionmaking to rank each country and then to reflect upon those rankings as it assesses its various arms trade options. This is reminiscent of the exporter's treatment of the political relations information. For other regions, such as the Middle East or the Persian

Gulf, the nation weights may not by themselves be significant, but they become so when values are provided for the political relations variables. The reason for this is easy to see. Specifying values for the political relations variables substantially reduces an exporter's ability to draw distinctions between countries. As discovered above, however, an exporter wishes to make such distinctions and seeks information that would allow it to do so. When that information is unavailable in the political relations variables, the exporter's only recourse is to turn to the nation weights. This is what is demonstrated by the Tukey comparisons of naive models 2 and 3. Boundary values are assigned to the political relations variables in both models, but only naive model 2 includes the nation weights. The presence of the nation weights must, therefore, be responsible for the significant differences that are consistently obtained between the two models.

Conclusion

The Tukey analyses are enormously instructive inasmuch as they demonstrate that hegemonic exporters thirst for information and that they process the information they are able to gather in an altogether rational manner. They also suggest that arms trade decisionmaking has been conceptualized properly in this research. The differences between the theoretical and naive models are purely a function of the way the utilities are envisioned. Since the theoretical model always performs significantly better than naive models 2 and 3, and since, in some instances, naive model 1 is also found to be deficient, it seems fair to say that the theoretical model's image of utility is nearest to real world circumstances. Hegemonic arms exporters make their policy choices only after evaluating the variable effects of each of their strategic options on the political relationships of a number of states. They seem particularly concerned about the impact of their options on their own relations, on relations involving their adversary, and on relations among the countries of the import region. All four models suggest that these are the subjects that matter to hegemonic exporters, which are, indeed, the substance of their utilities, but only the theoretical model allows for their fullest expression. Each of the naive models diminishes the values of the utilities by transforming one or both of its key components—i.e., w_j and the c variables—from variables to constants. These changes are not just statistically undesirable, as they are often shown to be, but they also have the effect of adulterating the meaning of the expected-utility model by limiting, even sometimes obviating, the exporter's ability to evaluate the potential impact of its strategies on the political relations of each individual actor. The exporter should be permitted to conduct the kinds of calculations that are proposed through the utilities of the theoretical model and that are demonstrated by the Tukey test results to be the ones the exporter wishes to make.

The genuinely large proportions that were obtained for most of the predictions of the theoretical model provide additional support for the way the policymaking process has been conceived. The statistically significant differences that were found between the theoretical and naive models in both the analyses of variance and Tukey tests would have been much less inspirational had the proportions for all of the models been substantially smaller. Scores, say, in the neighborhood of .500 for the theoretical model would have indicated that much of the arms export process had been left undeciphered. But this was not a problem, at least not for the first three regions. The theoretical model usually yielded proportions that were above .700 and often above .800, suggesting, once more, that the core concerns of hegemonic exporters were the political relationships specified in this research. Of course, none of this is especially surprising. That the United States and the Soviet Union would be interested chiefly in the impact of their arms export options on their own relations, on each other's relations, or on relations in the import region is a series of expectations that is supported not only by these empirical findings, but also by much anecdotal evidence. The truly interesting implication of the large proportions is that all of the other factors that are supposedly crucial ingredients of the policymaking process, such as, for example, the desire for economic gain or the dissemination of a particular ideology, are either less important than often thought or subsumed in the political relations lotteries. The same holds for those factors known to be important. Hegemonic exporters deliver weapons to Third World states to secure their own strategic positions, but the process through which an exporter might make a transfer decision on the basis of that factor appears to be no different from or, at the very least, adequately represented by the political relations lotteries of the model. In short, the expected-utility model initially proposed in this research is sufficiently flexible to capture most of the policymaking process.

These concluding comments only apply to the export practices of the United States and the Soviet Union, the two countries that SIPRI has labeled hegemonic exporters. This could be considered a limitation in that it ignores the potentially different behavior patterns of other exporters; but, rather than assessing it as such, the preference here is to acknowledge that SIPRI was probably correct to separate hegemonic exporters from those that it calls industrial and restrictive. Nothing can be said here about the accuracy of the processes that SIPRI presents for those other exporters, but if it is the case that a country like France delivers weapons *primarily* to keep its domestic arms industry running, or a country like Sweden supplies arms *chiefly* to ensure a peaceful import environment, then it is obvious that industrial and restrictive exporters adhere to processes that are markedly different from those of the United States and the Soviet Union. This is not to say, of course, that hegemonic exporters never make industrial or restrictive calculations; indeed, Lottery 4 of the arms trade model focuses on regional relations, which can be interpreted as a restrictive concern. The point is that hegemonic exporters have been shown to choose policies on the basis of factors that go beyond the proposed concerns of industrial and restrictive exporters, and in that respect, this project lends credence to SIPRI's view that arms trade policymaking probably differs among exporters.

Two countries for which the policymaking apparently does not differ are the United States and the Soviet Union. This point was made on several occasions in this chapter, so there is no need to belabor it here. In fact, it could even be argued that the correspondence between the superpowers was anticipated inasmuch as both were characterized as hegemonic exporters and treated in the same manner throughout this study. However, all of this seems to understate what has actually been discovered. The decisionmaking processes of the United States and the Soviet Union are not just similar; they match in almost every respect. This, quite frankly, was not anticipated. These are countries that embrace different principles, that find themselves supporting altogether different movements, and that recruit different kinds of Third World states as clients; they pursue, in short, different global political objectives. Moreover, they clash frequently over their differences, enough perhaps for one to expect some variation in the way they pursue their goals. But this is not the case, at least not as far as arms transfers are concerned. On each of the many indicators of comparison, the two countries demonstrate, time and again, that they make arms transfer decisions in essentially the same fashion. There were no appreciable differences between them over each of the first three regions. Even when there seemed to be some variation in one exporter's approach toward different importers, the same pattern was also exhibited by the other exporter. They were dependent upon the same kinds of political relations information, and they tended to gather that information from the same time periods. Similarities were also discovered between their processes for the three pairs of arms transfer strategies, even to the point where declines in predictive accuracy from one pair to another were at the same pace. Then there were the findings on the theoretical and naive models. Of all the measures of correspondence, these are certainly the most compelling. They indicate not only that the two countries were attentive to the political relations information proposed in this research, but also that they used that information in essentially the same way and that they suffered equivalent levels of inconvenience when portions of it were systematically eliminated from consideration. This is a tremendous record of agreement that clearly serves to emphasize that, during the years 1951–1976, the arms export practices of the United States and the Soviet Union were virtually identical for importers of the Middle East, the Persian Gulf, and South Asia.

The one region for which none of this applies is, of course, Central America. The proportions for the United States were uniformly low for each of the four expected-utility models, indicating that a large portion of the decisionmaking for that region was simply beyond the grasp of this project. Although it is impossible to state with certainty why this occurred, one plausible argument begins with the nature of the Central American environment. Unlike the other three regions,

Central America was usually designated noncompetitive-cooperative, and it was discovered that the submodel for that environment generated the smallest proportions for the region. The other three submodels functioned very well for the Middle East, the Persian Gulf, and South Asia, and the noncompetitive-conflictual submodel also performed well when it was employed for Central America. The region's overwhelmingly noncompetitive-cooperative status, which impelled a particular submodel to examine most of the decisionmaking, seemed the likely culprit for the poor results. And why does the submodel for the noncompetitive-cooperative environment operate so poorly? Perhaps because it is completely inattentive to the factors that concern arms importers.

Although this study focuses only on arms export decisionmaking, the other three submodels are at least indirectly alert to some of the issues—regional conflict, great power influence—that affect an importer's decision to seek arms. These number among the demand factors of the arms trade phenomenon, but the ones mentioned here are palpably less important to countries operating in noncompetitive settings. Those importers are probably motivated by other demand factors—perhaps internal security, or maybe the prestige or legitimacy that accompanies the acquisition of arms—and these are simply not addressed by the noncompetitive-cooperative submodel. All of this points to an important limitation of this research. To say that the expected-utility model performs well actually means that the noncompetitive-conflictual, competitive-cooperative, and competitive-conflictual versions of that model are able to capture arms export decisionmaking. The noncompetitive-cooperative submodel, on the other hand, is noticeably deficient, and the condition that distinguishes that submodel from the others is that it pertains to environments that happen to be stable. This assumes, of course, that superpower competition and conflictual regional relations are indicators of an unstable import environment. If that is agreed, then the expected-utility model proposed in this project is most representative of the decisionmaking for unstable regions.

Predicting strategies for Central America's noncompetitive-cooperative environment was one of two areas in which the expected-utility model was found lacking. The other area was the identification of exporter-to-importer strategies that fluctuated fairly regularly over time. The inability of the model to meet this challenge cast a pall over what was otherwise a promising set of findings. To be sure, the model was not totally deficient on this matter; the relatively dismal results for the difficult cases of the Middle East were counterbalanced, for example, by findings that were much better for comparable dyads of the Persian Gulf and South Asia. But, the fact remains that not one of the proportions that were pronounced satisfactory reached the appealing .800 plateau, and most were still at some distance from the proportions obtained for all the other dyads.

Several factors could conceivably be responsible for this discrepancy: the functional form of the model may be incorrect, the indices for the variables may be imprecise, the data used to measure the variables may be incomplete, and so on. In fact, each of these factors probably contributed to the problem, and they need not have been excessive for the problem to have emerged. An exporter's decision to change strategies for an importer from one year to the next could be motivated by the most subtle event or calculation, which means that the model, together with its operational instruments, must be able to grasp the particulars of an arms trade setting if it is to detect a shift in policy. This is a stiff requirement that apparently stretches the expected-utility model to its limits. The functional form, the operational rules and indices, and the data for the variables were all sufficient for the routine policymaking case, but they could not capture all the shades and nuances of an exporter's deliberations, and it is for this reason that the model had some difficulty predicting strategies for certain dyads.

Still, the limitations of a major research effort should never be allowed to disguise what is actually achieved. It seems reasonable to close on an upbeat note by emphasizing once again that the expected-utility model effectively represents much of the arms export process. This is no mean accomplishment. Many thoughtful researchers are of the opinion that theory and arms transfers are legions apart. Consider, for example, the trenchant words of Neuman and Harkavy (1980, 315):

> No explicit attempt was here made to uncover a "theory" of arms transfers. The subject is quite probably of a complexity well beyond

the level where one might contemplate tight causal models, and explicitly set forth formal relationships between sets of dependent and independent variables.

If nothing else, this study should put an end to expressions of this kind. Arms transfers may indeed be complex phenomena, but they are not so complex as to foreclose the possibility of theoretical and empirical inquiry. A few simplifying assumptions regarding the actors and their goals are generally enough to begin the process of thinking theoretically. In this study, for example, all of the various public and private subnational actors that are usually involved in the decisionmaking (at least for the United States), together with the issues and interests that typically inspire them, were unceremoniously ignored and, judging by the results, their absence was not especially debilitating. Of course, the success of this or any other theoretical undertaking is also dependent upon the modeling mechanism. Expected-utility theory was chosen for this project because it conceived of decisionmaking as a rational, value-maximizing enterprise, and because it promised to contend with actor uncertainty. The preponderance of the evidence reported in this chapter clearly indicates that the technique has fulfilled its promise. Expected-utility theory is indeed applicable to the arms transfer subject.

Appendix

Exporter-to-Importer Proportions for the Naive Models[a]

	United States			Soviet Union		
	N1	N2	N3	N1	N2	N3
Middle East						
Export/No Export						
Egypt	.923	.885	.346	.615	.423	.192
Israel	.923	.885	.308	.962	.731	.654
Jordan	.769	.808	.385	.923	.577	.346
Lebanon	.654	.654	.385	.769	.500	.346
Syria	.962	.846	.500	.692	.462	.231
	($t1;N=26$)[a]			($t1;N=26$)		
Increase/Decrease						
Egypt	.880	.720	.320	.520	.600	.520
Israel	.440	.440	.480	.960	.640	.600
Jordan	.560	.640	.640	.920	.440	.280
Lebanon	.640	.640	.520	.760	.480	.360
Syria	.960	.800	.400	.440	.520	.520
	($t2;N=25$)			($t2;N=25$)		
High/Low						
Egypt	.917	.708	.291	.542	.625	.458
Israel	.583	.583	.542	.958	.667	.625
Jordan	.625	.625	.542	.917	.417	.250
Lebanon	.625	.625	.500	.750	.458	.333
Syria	.958	.792	.375	.375	.458	.458
	($t2;N=24$)			($t2;N=24$)		
Persian Gulf						
Export/No Export						
Iran	.769	.654	.423	.500	.615	.385
Iraq	.923	.692	.614	.692	.691	.500
Kuwait	.846	.731	.577	.846	.885	.769
Saudi Arabia	.654	.654	.615	.846	.923	.808
	($t1;N=26$)			($t2;N=26$)		
Increase/Decrease						
Iran	.680	.760	.720	.458	.625	.375
Iraq	.800	.560	.600	.750	.792	.833
Kuwait	.840	.720	.760	.792	.833	.708
Saudi Arabia	.600	.440	.520	.750	.833	.708
	($t1;N=25$)			($t3;N=24$)		
High/Low						
Iran	.667	.708	.625	.583	.542	.333
Iraq	.875	.667	.583	.833	.708	.625
Kuwait	.875	.750	.583	.875	.833	.792
Saudi Arabia	.667	.625	.667	.875	.833	.792
	($t1;N=24$)			($t1;N=24$)		

(continued overleaf)

(continued)

	United States			Soviet Union		
	N1	N2	N3	N1	N2	N3
South Asia						
Export/No Export						
Afghanistan	.885	.769	.385	.615	.615	.615
India	.654	.538	.500	.769	.385	.423
Nepal	.923	.692	.462	.769	.731	.692
Pakistan	.692	.538	.423	.808	.577	.538
Sri Lanka	.769	.808	.462	.808	.769	.654
		$(t1; N = 26)$			$(t2; N = 26)$	
Increase/Decrease						
Afghanistan	.760	.800	.520	.458	.708	.792
India	.680	.560	.480	.542	.500	.625
Nepal	.640	680	.400	.708	.667	.625
Pakistan	.640	.640	.520	.833	.500	458
Sri Lanka	.800	.840	.640	.750	.708	.583
		$(t2; N = 25)$			$(t3; N = 24)$	
High/Low						
Afghanistan	.708	.750	.500	.667	.750	.667
India	.625	.583	.458	.583	.625	.667
Nepal	.667	.708	.417	.708	.667	.625
Pakistan	.667	.667	.500	.875	.500	.458
Sri Lanka	.708	.750	.542	.833	.792	.667
		$(t2; N = 24)$			$(t2; N = 24)$	
Central America						
Export/No Export						
Costa Rica	.480	.480	.520	.885	.885	.885
El Salvador	.600	.520	.480	.923	.923	.885
Guatemala	.520	.520	.520	.923	.962	.885
Honduras	.320	.320	.320	1.000	1.000	1.000
Nicaragua	.760	.760	.720	1.000	1.000	1.000
Panama	.520	.400	.400	.962	1.000	.962
		$(t3; N = 25)$.			$(t1 \text{ or } t2; N = 26)$	
Increase/Decrease						
Costa Rica	.458	.458	.500	.880	.880	.880
El Salvador	.583	.500	.458	.920	.920	.880
Guatemala	.542	.417	.417	.920	.960	.880
Honduras	.458	.417	.417	1.000	1.000	1.000
Nicaragua	.667	.667	.625	1.000	1.000	1.000
Panama	.542	.458	.458	.960	1.000	.960
		$(t3; N = 24)$			$(t1 \text{ or } t2; N = 25)$	
High/Low						
Costa Rica	.542	.500	.500	.875	.875	.875
El Salvador	.667	.583	.583	.917	.917	.875
Guatemala	.500	.542	.542	.917	.958	.875
Honduras	.750	.625	.583	1.000	1.000	1.000
Nicaragua	.708	.667	.667	1.000	1.000	1.000
Panama	.625	.542	.500	.958	1.000	.958
		$(t1; N = 24)$			$(t1 \text{ or } t2; N = 24)$	

[a]The Ns and time period options located underneath a block of proportions apply to each proportion within the block.

References

Agwani, Mohammed S. 1978. *Politics in the Gulf.* New Delhi: Vikas Publishing House.

Alpert, Eugene J. 1976. "Capabilities, Perceptions, and Risks: A Bayesian Model of International Behavior." *International Studies Quarterly* 20: 415–440.

Ambrose, Stephen E. 1985, 6th rev. ed. *Rise to Globalism: American Foreign Policy Since 1938.* New York: Penguin Books.

Ameringer, Charles D. 1982. *Democracy in Costa Rica.* New York: Praeger Publishers.

Anthony, John D. 1981. "The Persian Gulf in Regional and International Politics: the Arab Side of the Gulf." In *The Security of the Persian Gulf,* H. Amirsadeghi, ed., pp. 170–196. New York: St. Martin's Press.

Azar, Edward E. 1982. *The Codebook of the Conflict and Peace Data Bank (COPDAB): A Computer Assisted Approach to Monitoring and Analyzing International and Domestic Events.* University of North Carolina, Chapel Hill.

———. 1980. The Conflict and Peace Data Bank (COPDAB) Project. *Journal of Conflict Resolution* 24: 143–152.

Barnds, William J. 1972. *India, Pakistan, and the Great Powers.* New York: Praeger Publishers.

Bueno de Mesquita, Bruce. 1980. "An Expected Utility Theory of International Conflict." *American Political Science Review* 74: 917–931.

———. 1981. *The War Trap.* New Haven: Yale University Press.

Burke, S. M. 1973. *Pakistan's Foreign Policy: An Historical Analysis*. London: Oxford University Press.

Campbell, John C. 1972. "The Soviet Union and the United States in the Middle East." *Annals of the American Academy of Political and Social Science* 401: 126–135.

Chawla, Sudershan. 1976. *The Foreign Relations of India*. Encino: Dickenson Publishing Company.

Choudhury, Golam W. 1968. *Pakistan's Relations with India, 1947–1966*. New York: Praeger Publishers.

Chubin, Shahram. 1982. *Security in the Persian Gulf: The Role of Outside Powers*. New York: International Institute for Strategic Studies.

Frank, Lewis A. 1969. *The Arms Trade in International Relations*. New York: Praeger Publishers.

Gallhofer, I. N. and W. E. Saris. 1979. "Strategy Choices of Foreign Policy Decision Makers: The Netherlands, 1914." *Journal of Conflict Resolution* 23: 425–445.

Haass, Richard. 1981. "Saudi Arabia and Iran: The Twin Pillars in Revolutionary Times." In *The Security of the Persian Gulf*, H. Amirsadeghi, ed., pp. 151–169. New York: St. Martin's Press.

Harkavy, Robert E. 1980. "The New Geopolitics: Arms Transfers and the Major Powers' Competition for Overseas Bases." In *Arms Transfers in the Modern World*, S. G. Neuman and R. E. Harkavy, eds., pp. 131–151. New York: Praeger Publishers.

Hayes, Margaret D. 1982. "United States Security Interests in Central America in Global Perspective." In *Central America: International Dimensions of the Crisis*, R. E. Feinberg, ed., pp. 85–102. New York: Holmes & Meier Publishers, Inc.

International Monetary Fund. 1981. *Direction of Trade*. Published annually.

Kaplan, Stephen S. 1975. "U.S. Arms Transfers to Latin America, 1945–1974: Rational Strategy, Bureaucratic Politics, and Executive Parameters." *International Studies Quarterly* 19: 399–431.

Kemp, Geoffrey with Steven Miller. 1979. "The Arms Transfer Phenomenon." In *Arms Transfers and American Foreign Policy*, A. Pierre, ed., pp. 15–97. New York: New York University Press.

Khalilzad, Zalmay. 1982. "Soviet Policies in West Asia and

the Persian Gulf." In *Soviet Foreign Policy in the 1980s*, R. E. Kanet, ed., pp. 312–329. New York: Praeger Publishers.

Kolodziej, Edward A. 1980. "Arms Transfers and International Politics: The Interdependence of Independence." In *Arms Transfers in the Modern World*, S. G. Neuman and R. E. Harkavy, eds., pp. 3–26. New York: Praeger Publishers.

Kramer, Francisco V. 1982. "The Background of the Current Political Crisis in Central America." In *Central America: International Dimensions of the Crisis*, R. E. Feinberg, ed., pp. 15–35. New York: Holmes & Meier Publishers, Inc.

LaFeber, Walter. 1984. *Inevitable Revolutions: The United States in Central America*. New York: W. W. Norton & Company.

Lenczowki, George. 1981. *The Middle East in World Affairs*. Ithaca: Cornell University Press.

Luce, R. Duncan and Howard Raiffa. 1957. *Games and Decisions*. New York: Wiley.

McLaurin, Ronald D. 1977. "Soviet Policy in the Persian Gulf." In *Conflict and Cooperation in the Gulf*, M. Mughisuddin, ed., pp. 116–139. New York: Praeger Publishers.

Mintz, Alex. 1980. *Strategic Competitors, Military Capability Builders, and the Structure of the International System: An Empirical Analysis of Arms Transfers to Eight Pairs of Developing Nations*, 1960–1980. Unpublished manuscript.

Neter, John and William Wasserman. 1971. *Applied Linear Statistical Models*. Homewood: Richard D. Irwin, Inc.

Neuman, Stephanie G. and Robert E. Harkavy. 1980. "The Road to Further Research and Theory in Arms Transfers." In *Arms Transfers in the Modern World*, S. G. Neuman and R. E. Harkavy, eds., pp. 315–321. New York: Praeger Publishers.

Ramazani, Rouhallah K. 1975. *Iran's Foreign Policy, 1941–1973: A Study of Foreign Policy in Modernizing Nations*. Charlottesville: University Press of Virginia.

Rudolph, James D. 1983. *Honduras: A Country Study*. Washington, D.C.: U. S. Government Printing Office.

Sanjian, Gregory S., forthcoming. "Expected-Utility Theory

and Arms Transfers: A Model of Export Decision-making." In *The State as Actor: Merriam: Seminar Series on Research Frontiers*, D. Zinnes, ed. Denver, University of Denver.

Schrodt, Philip A. 1982. *Contagion Effect in Arms Transfers: A Statistical Study*. Paper presented at the annual meeting of the International Studies Association, Cincinatti, Ohio.

Sella, Amnon. 1981. *Soviet Political and Military Conduct in the Middle East*. New York: St. Martin's Press.

Starr, Harvey and Benjamin A. Most. 1976. "The Substance and Study of Borders in International Relations." *International Studies Quarterly* 20: 581–620.

Stockholm International Peace Research Institute (SIPRI). 1971. *The Arms Trade with the Third World*. London: Paul Elek Limited.

Stockholm International Peace Research Institute (SIPRI). 1975. *Arms Trade Registers: The Arms Trade with the Third World*. Cambridge: Massachusetts Institute of Technology.

U. S. Arms Control and Disarmament Agency. 1984. *World Military Expenditures and Arms Transfers, 1972–82*. Washington, D.C.: U. S. Government Printing Office.

Woodward, Ralph L. 1976. *Central America: A Nation Divided*. New York: Oxford University Press.

Index

About the Book and the Author

Professor Sanjian develops and tests an expected-utility model of arms transfer decisionmaking, focusing on the activities of a hegemonic exporter—a country that chooses an arms strategy toward a prospective importer only after evaluating the political and strategic consequences of all its options. He identifies three factors as having potentially the greatest impact on an exporter's choice of strategy: (1) the extent to which there is conflict between the prospective importer and all of its neighbors; (2) the exporter's relationships with the countries of the import region (including, of course, the prospective importer); and (3) the degree of competition between the exporter and its geopolitical rival for influence in the import region. These decisionmaking criteria are incorporated in the model's four expected-utility lotteries.

The model is tested by predicting the arms strategies of the two superpowers for several Third World importers during 1951–1976 and by comparing the accuracy of those predictions with the performances of three naive models. The tests reveal that arms trade policymaking is represented best by the expected-utility model and that the process itself is remarkably consistent over a number of critical values.

Gregory S. Sanjian is assistant professor of political science at Bucknell University. His current research focuses on the area of arms transfers, particularly probabilistic and possibilistic models of the decisionmaking process and the effects of arms transfers on regional conflict and stability.